Presented to

Mark, Richie, DaviD
Jhon others, timothey
and luke

By

Alex

On the Occasion of

chrismas

Date

1/19/03

JESUS
from A to Z

SELECTED BIBLE VERSES FOR KNOWING HIM BETTER

AMY NG WONG

BARBOUR
PUBLISHING, INC.
Uhrichsville, Ohio

Published by Barbour Publishing, Inc., P.O. Box 719, Uhrichsville, Ohio 44683 http://www.barbourbooks.com

 Member of the
Evangelical Christian
Publishers Association

Printed in the United States of America.

Acknowledgments

Thank you Bible Study Fellowship, International, for seeking the Lord in all that you do. Thank you for your desire for people around the world to know God and to know the Lord Jesus Christ, through the knowledge of His Word in the Bible and through obedience to His precepts.

But most important, through this obedience, when we have experienced the truth of God's precepts and His presence, we know that He is worthy, we know that we can freely love Him with all our heart, all our soul, all our mind, and all our strength.

CONTENTS

PREFACE

Amazing, Baptizer, Compassionate,
Dependable, Exalted, Faithful,
Generous, Humble, Innocent,
Justifier, Kind, Light, Merciful, Near,
Overcomer, Passionate, Quiet,
Rewarder, Sinless, Trustworthy,
Unchanging, Vine, Willing, Xristos,
Yearning, Zealous

If I knew a man with these attributes—or even just a few of them—I would fall head over heels, completely and absolutely in love with him! I would want to marry him. Any man who might know a woman with some of these attributes would want to marry her.

There is a Person who exhibits every one of these qualities—Jesus. And if we love Him with all our heart, soul, and strength, we will marry that perfect person—because Jesus Christ will be the bridegroom, and we will be His bride (see Matthew 25:1–10, Revelation 19:7–8)!

This book contains hundreds of Bible verses that describe the character qualities, or attributes, of Jesus. You'll be amazed as you meet Him in all His power, glory, and love—as you meet Jesus, from A to Z.

Note: The verses used in this book have been carefully selected from a number of Bible translations—whichever translation best brought out the attribute of Jesus under consideration. In some Bible versions, "thee," "thou," and "thine" mean "you" and "yours." "Ye" means "you." In this book, italicized type indicates material added by the author to clarify or explain Bible passages.

JESUS. . .A

Almighty

See! He is arriving, surrounded by clouds; and every eye shall see him—yes, and those who pierced him *(those responsible for nailing him on the cross)*. And the nations will weep in sorrow and in terror when he comes. Yes! Amen! Let it be so! "I am the A and the Z, the Beginning and the Ending of all things," says God, who is the Lord, the All Powerful One who is, and was, and is coming again!

REVELATION 1:7–8 TLB

Alpha

"I am the Alpha and the Omega, the Beginning and the End," says the Lord, "who is and who was and who is to come, the Almighty."

REVELATION 1:8 NKJV

Amazing

All who heard it were amazed at what the shepherds told them.   LUKE 2:18 NRSV

Ambassador

And this is eternal life: to have knowledge of you, the only true God, and of him whom you have sent, even Jesus Christ.   JOHN 17:3 BBE

Jesus explains, "For I have come down from heaven, not to do My own will, but the will of Him who sent Me."   JOHN 6:38 NKJV

And he [Jesus] said to them, You are of the earth; I am from heaven: you are of this world; I am not of this world.   JOHN 8:23 BBE

Jesus said to them, "Very truly, I tell you, the Son can do nothing on his own, but only what he sees the Father doing; for whatever the Father does, the Son does likewise."

JOHN 5:19 NRSV

Jesus came to earth to represent God, to accomplish God's will, to help us know God, and to help each one of us establish a personal relationship with the LORD.

Jesus answered, "My teaching is not my own. It comes from him who sent me. If anyone chooses to do God's will, he will find out whether my teaching comes from God or whether I speak on my own. He who speaks on his own does so to gain honor for himself, but he who works for the honor of the one who sent him is a man of truth; there is nothing false about him."

JOHN 7:16–18 NIV

Authority

Now when Jesus had finished saying these things, the crowds were astounded at his teaching, for he taught them as one having authority, and not as their scribes.

MATTHEW 7:28–29 NRSV

And Jesus came and spoke to them, saying, "All authority has been given to Me in heaven and on earth." MATTHEW 28:18 NKJV

See, I have given you *(who believe and follow Jesus)* power to put your feet on snakes and evil beasts, and over all the strength of him who is against you: and nothing will do you damage. Do not be glad, however, because you have power over spirits, but because your names are recorded in heaven. LUKE 10:19–20 BBE

We should rejoice in who we are in Christ, not in what we do because of the power He gives us.

God put this power to work in Christ when he raised him from the dead and seated him at his right hand in the heavenly places, far above all rule and authority and power and dominion, and above every name that is named, not only in this age but also in the age to come. And he has put all things under his feet and has made him the head over all things for the church, which is his body, the fullness of him who fills all in all.   EPHESIANS 1:20–23 NRSV

Awesome

From the west, men will fear the name of the LORD, and from the rising of the sun, they will revere his glory. For he will come like a pent-up flood that the breath of the LORD drives along.
ISAIAH 59:19 NIV

JESUS. . .B

Baptizer

"I baptize you with water for repentance, but one [Jesus] who is more powerful than I is coming after me; I am not worthy to carry his sandals. He will baptize you with the Holy Spirit and fire." MATTHEW 3:11 NRSV

See attributes of God the Holy Spirit, "Baptism," for definition or impact of being baptized.

Beginning

And he also said, "It is finished! I am the Alpha and the Omega—the Beginning and the End. To all who are thirsty I will give the springs of the water of life without charge!"

REVELATION 21:6 NLT

In the beginning was the Word, and the Word was with God, and the Word was God. He was in the beginning with God.   JOHN 1:1–2 RSV

(The "Word" here is Jesus. See the "Word" attribute of God the Son.)

He is before all things, and in him all things have being.   COLOSSIANS 1:17 BBE

Branch

"Now listen, Joshua, high priest, you and your colleagues who sit before you! For they are an omen of things to come: I am going to bring my servant the Branch."   ZECHARIAH 3:8 NRSV

In those days and at that time I will cause to grow up to David a Branch of righteousness; He shall execute judgment and righteousness in the earth. In those days Judah will be saved, and Jerusalem will dwell safely. And this is the name by which she will be called: THE LORD OUR RIGHTEOUSNESS.

JEREMIAH 33:15–16 NKJV

And there will come a rod out of the broken tree of Jesse, and a branch out of his roots will give fruit. And the spirit of the Lord will be resting on him, the spirit of wisdom and good sense, the spirit of wise guiding and strength, the spirit of knowledge and of the fear of the Lord; And he will not be guided in his judging by what he sees, or give decisions by the hearing of his ears: But he will do right in the cause of the poor, and give wise decisions for those in the land who are in need; and the rod of his mouth will come down on the cruel, and with the breath of his lips he will put an end to the evil-doer.   ISAIAH 11:1–4 BBE

In that day the Branch of the LORD shall be beautiful and glorious.   ISAIAH 4:2 NKJV

"Thus says the LORD of hosts, saying: 'Behold, the Man whose name is the BRANCH! From His place He shall branch out, and He shall build the temple of the LORD.' "   ZECHARIAH 6:12 NKJV

Bread

Jesus said, "Moses didn't give it *(the bread from heaven)* to them. My Father did. And now he offers you true Bread from heaven. The true Bread is a Person—the one sent by God from heaven, and he gives life to the world."

JOHN 6:32–33 TLB

And this was the answer of Jesus: I am the bread of life. He who comes to me will never be in need of food, and he who has faith in me will never be in need of drink.   JOHN 6:35 BBE

Bridegroom

"Then the kingdom of heaven will be like this. Ten bridesmaids took their lamps and went to meet the bridegroom."   MATTHEW 25:1 NRSV

"Let us rejoice and exult and give him the glory, for the marriage of the Lamb has come, and his bride has made herself ready; to her it has been granted to be clothed with fine linen, bright and pure"—for the fine linen is the righteous deeds of the saints.   REVELATION 19:7–8 NRSV

The Lamb is Jesus, and His bride is the church—all the people who love Him. The bright pure linen represents our righteous acts done through faith in Him.

I feel a divine jealousy for you, for I promised you in marriage to one husband, to present you as a chaste virgin to Christ.

2 CORINTHIANS 11:2 NRSV

Brother
See "Family."

We who have been made holy by Jesus, now have the same Father he has. That is why Jesus is not ashamed to call us his brothers. For he says in the book of Psalms, "I will talk to my brothers about God my Father, and together we will sing his praises."   HEBREWS 2:11–12 TLB

For we know, brothers and sisters beloved by God, that he has chosen you, because our message of the gospel came to you not in word only, but also in power and in the Holy Spirit and with full conviction.   1 THESSALONIANS 1:4 NRSV

JESUS. . .C

Caring

He will bring justice to the poor of the people; He will save the children of the needy, and will break in pieces the oppressor.   PSALM 72:4 NKJV

He will rescue the poor when they cry to him; he will help the oppressed, who have no one to defend them. He feels pity for the weak and the needy, and he will rescue them. He will save them from oppression and from violence, for their lives are precious to him.   PSALM 72:12–14 NLT

The crushed stem will not be broken by him; and the feebly burning light will he not put out, till he has made righteousness overcome all.

MATTHEW 12:20 BBE

Even when people seem hopelessly lost to sin or evil, Jesus will still not give up on them.

When the Lord saw her, his heart overflowed with compassion. "Don't cry!" he said.

LUKE 7:13 NLT

Cast all your anxiety on him, because he cares for you.   1 PETER 5:7 NRSV

Christ

Christ is God's son, God's greatest expression and action of love for us even while we were yet His enemies (sinners).

For God had such love for the world that he gave his only Son, so that whoever has faith in him may not come to destruction but have eternal life.   JOHN 3:16 BBE

But God proves his love for us in that while we still were sinners Christ died for us.

ROMANS 5:8 NRSV

Would you die for an enemy, or die for someone who doesn't even know you?

"Now salvation, and strength, and the kingdom of our God, and the power of His Christ have come." REVELATION 12:10 NKJV

Compassionate

But when He saw the multitudes, He was moved with compassion for them, because they were weary and scattered, like sheep having no shepherd. MATTHEW 9:36 NKJV

Jesus wept. JOHN 11:35 RSV

"For I was hungry and you gave me food, I was thirsty and you gave me drink, I was a stranger and you welcomed me, I was naked and you clothed me, I was sick and you visited me, I was in prison and you came to me."

MATTHEW 25:35–36 RSV

Jesus is so compassionate that when we help others, He considers it as if we had done it for Him personally!

People were bringing even infants to him that he might touch them; and when the disciples saw it, they sternly ordered them not to do it. But Jesus called for them and said, "Let the little children come to me, and do not stop them; for it is to such as these that the kingdom of God belongs." LUKE 18:15–16 NRSV

Now a leper came to Him, imploring Him, kneeling down to Him and saying to Him, "If You are willing, You can make me clean." Then Jesus, moved with compassion, stretched out His hand and touched him, and said to him, "I am willing; be cleansed." MARK 1:40–41 NKJV

Lepers were considered unclean and untouchable; they were separated from everyone else. Anyone touching a leper would also become unclean. Jesus was so compassionate that He considered the person as more important than the law—and more important than Himself. He touched the unclean, to meet the leper where he was. Jesus Christ became sin for us, although He Himself knew no sin, that we might be made the righteousness of God in Him.

"These are they who have come out of the great tribulation; they have washed their robes and made them white in the blood of the Lamb [Jesus]. . . . Never again will they hunger; never again will they thirst. The sun will not beat upon them, nor any scorching heat. For the Lamb [Jesus] at the center of the throne will be their shepherd; he will lead them to springs of living water. And God will wipe away every tear from their eyes."   REVELATION 7:14–17 NIV

Constant

Jesus Christ is the same yesterday and today and for ever.   HEBREWS 13:8 RSV

Cornerstone

" 'The stone that the builders rejected has become the cornerstone; this was the Lord's doing, and it is amazing in our eyes'. . . . The one who falls on this stone will be broken to pieces; and it will crush anyone on whom it falls."

MATTHEW 21:42, 44 NRSV

"See, I am laying in Zion a stone, a cornerstone chosen and precious; and whoever believes in him will not be put to shame." 1 PETER 2:6 NRSV

Jesus, symbolized as the cornerstone which determines where a building is to be built, is the most important stone in God's building. We who love Jesus are the individual stones stemming from the cornerstone, being used to build the spiritual building.

As you come to him, the living Stone—rejected by men but chosen by God and precious to him—you also, like living stones, are being built into a spiritual house to be a holy priesthood, offering spiritual sacrifices acceptable to God through Jesus Christ. 1 PETER 2:4–5 NIV

Now therefore ye are no more strangers and foreigners, but fellowcitizens with the saints, and of the household of God; and are built upon the foundation of the apostles and prophets, Jesus Christ himself being the chief corner stone; in whom all the building fitly framed together groweth unto an holy temple in the Lord: In whom ye also are builded together for an habitation of God through the Spirit.

EPHESIANS 2:19–22 KJV

Counselor

For unto us a Child is born, unto us a Son is given; and the government will be upon His shoulder. And His name will be called Wonderful, Counselor, Mighty God, Everlasting Father, Prince of Peace. Of the increase of His government and peace there will be no end.

ISAIAH 9:6–7 NKJV

"Every one who comes to me and hears my words and does them, I will show you what he is like: he is like a man building a house, who dug deep, and laid the foundation upon rock; and when a flood arose, the stream broke against that house, and could not shake it, because it had been well built. But he who hears and does not do them is like a man who built a house on the ground without a foundation; against which the stream broke, and immediately it fell, and the ruin of that house was great." LUKE 6:47–49 RSV

Creator

But we know that there is only one God, the Father, who created everything, and we exist for him. And there is only one Lord, Jesus Christ, through whom God made everything and through whom we have been given life.

1 CORINTHIANS 8:6 NLT

Before anything else existed, there was Christ, with God. He has always been alive and is himself God. He created everything there is—nothing exists that he didn't make.

JOHN 1:1–3 TLB

He is the image of the invisible God, the firstborn of all creation; for in him all things were created, in heaven and on earth, visible and invisible, whether thrones or dominions or principalities or authorities—all things were created through him and for him.

COLOSSIANS 1:15–16 RSV

God, who at various times and in various ways spoke in time past to the fathers by the prophets, has in these last days spoken to us by His Son, whom He has appointed heir of all things, through whom also He made the worlds.

HEBREWS 1:1–2 NKJV

"You, LORD, in the beginning laid the foundation of the earth, and the heavens are the work of Your hands. They will perish, but You remain; and they will all grow old like a garment; like a cloak You will fold them up, and they will be changed. But You are the same, and Your years will not fail."

HEBREWS 1:10–12, PSALM 102:25–27 NKJV

JESUS. . .D

Defender

But if anybody does sin, we have one who speaks to the Father in our defense—Jesus Christ, the Righteous One.   1 JOHN 2:1 NIV

My little children, I am writing these things to you so that you may be without sin. And if any man is a sinner, we have a friend and helper with the Father, Jesus Christ, the upright one.

1 JOHN 2:1 BBE

He is able, once and forever, to save everyone who comes to God through him. He lives forever to plead with God on their behalf.

HEBREWS 7:25 NLT

Deity

For in Christ there is all of God in a human body; so you have everything when you have Christ, and you are filled with God through your union with Christ. He is the highest Ruler, with authority over every other power.

COLOSSIANS 2:9–10 TLB

Christ is the exact likeness of the unseen God. He existed before God made anything at all, and, in fact, Christ himself is the Creator who made everything in heaven and earth, the things we can see and the things we can't; the spirit world with its kings and kingdoms, its rulers and authorities; all were made by Christ.

COLOSSIANS 1:15–16 TLB

Dependable

My sheep hear my voice, and I know them, and they follow me: And I give unto them eternal life; and they shall never perish, neither shall any man pluck them out of my hand. My Father, which gave them me, is greater than all;

and no man is able to pluck them out of my Father's hand. I and my Father are one.

JOHN 10:27–30 KJV

And I am convinced that nothing can ever separate us from his love. Death can't, and life can't. The angels can't, and the demons can't. Our fears for today, our worries about tomorrow, and even the powers of hell can't keep God's love away. Whether we are high above the sky or in the deepest ocean, nothing in all creation will ever be able to separate us from the love of God that is revealed in Christ Jesus our Lord.

ROMANS 8:38–39 NLT

Dependent

As the living Father has sent me, and I have life because of the Father, even so he who takes me for his food will have life because of me.

JOHN 6:57 BBE

Jesus said to them, "If God were your Father, you would love Me, for I proceeded forth and came from God; nor have I come of Myself, but He sent Me."

JOHN 8:42 NKJV

"Don't you believe that I am in the Father and the Father is in me? The words I say are not my own, but my Father who lives in me does his work through me." JOHN 14:10 NLT

"Now they know that everything I have is a gift from you [the Father]." JOHN 17:7 TLB

Diligent

Jesus asked, "Why did you seek Me? Did you not know that I must be about My Father's business?" LUKE 2:49 NKJV

But there are also many other things which Jesus did; were every one of them to be written, I suppose that the world itself could not contain the books that would be written. JOHN 21:25 RSV

Discerning

Jesus knew their thoughts.

MATTHEW 12:25 NKJV

And the spirit of the LORD shall rest upon him, the spirit of wisdom and understanding, the spirit of counsel and might, the spirit of knowledge and of the fear of the LORD; and shall make him of quick understanding in the fear of the LORD: and he shall not judge after the sight of his eyes, neither reprove after the hearing of his ears: But with righteousness shall he judge the poor, and reprove with equity for the meek of the earth: and he shall smite the earth: with the rod of his mouth, and with the breath of his lips shall he slay the wicked. And righteousness shall be the girdle of his loins, and faithfulness the girdle of his reins.　　　ISAIAH 11:2–5 KJV

For the word of God is full of living power. It is sharper than the sharpest knife, cutting deep into our innermost thoughts and desires. It exposes us for what we really are.

HEBREWS 4:12 NLT

The "Word of God" is the Bible as well as Jesus— "The Word became flesh" (John 1:14).

JESUS. . .E

Encourager

Now our Lord Jesus Christ himself, and God our Father who had love for us and has given us eternal comfort and good hope through grace, give you comfort and strength in every good work and word.   2 THESSALONIANS 2:16–17 BBE

Exalted

For it was fitting that we should have such a high priest [Jesus], holy, blameless, undefiled, separated from sinners, and exalted above the heavens.   HEBREWS 7:26 NRSV

And being found in fashion as a man, he humbled himself, and became obedient unto death, even the death of the cross. Wherefore God also hath highly exalted him, and given him a name which is above every name: That at the name of Jesus every knee should bow, of things in heaven, and things in earth, and things under the earth; and that every tongue should confess that Jesus Christ is Lord, to the glory of God the Father.   PHILIPPIANS 2:8–11 KJV

Excellent

Yes, everything else is worthless when compared with the priceless gain of knowing Christ Jesus my Lord. I have discarded everything else, counting it all as garbage, so that I may have Christ and become one with him.   PHILIPPIANS 3:8 NLT

JESUS. . .F

Faithful

Christ, however, was faithful over God's house as a son, and we are his house if we hold firm the confidence and the pride that belong to hope.

HEBREWS 3:6 NRSV

Therefore, dear brothers whom God has set apart for himself—you who are chosen for heaven—I want you to think now about this Jesus who is God's Messenger and the High Priest of our faith. For Jesus was faithful to God who appointed him High Priest, just as Moses also faithfully served in God's house.

HEBREWS 3:1–2 TLB

"Let not your heart be troubled; you believe in God, believe also in Me. In My Father's house are many mansions; if it were not so, I would have told you. I go to prepare a place for you. And if I go and prepare a place for you, I will come again and receive you to Myself; that where I am, there you may be also." JOHN 14:1–3 NKJV

But the Lord is faithful; he will strengthen you and guard you from evil.

2 THESSALONIANS 3:3 RSV

And from Jesus Christ, the faithful witness, the firstborn from the dead, and the ruler over the kings of the earth. REVELATION 1:5 NKJV

Family

Jesus explains, "For whoever does the will of God is My brother and My sister and mother."

MARK 3:35 NKJV

For the one who sanctifies and those who are sanctified all have one Father. For this reason Jesus is not ashamed to call them brothers and sisters. HEBREWS 2:11 NRSV

For ye are all the children of God by faith in Christ Jesus. For as many of you as have been baptized into Christ have put on Christ. There is neither Jew nor Greek, there is neither bond nor free, there is neither male nor female: for ye are all one in Christ Jesus.   GALATIANS 3:26–28 KJV

Famous

"And at the Judgment Day the Queen of Sheba shall arise and point her finger at this generation, condemning it, for she went on a long, hard journey to listen to the wisdom of Solomon; but one far greater than Solomon is here *(and few pay any attention)*."   LUKE 11:31 TLB

"The people of Nineveh, too, will rise up against this generation on judgment day and condemn it, because they repented at the preaching of Jonah. And now someone greater than Jonah is here—and you refuse to repent."

LUKE 11:32 NLT

Then He went out again by the sea; and all the multitude came to Him, and He taught them.

MARK 2:13 NKJV

Hearing all that he [Jesus] was doing, they came to him in great numbers from Judea, Jerusalem, Idumea, beyond the Jordan, and the region around Tyre and Sidon.   MARK 3:8 NRSV

At daybreak he departed and went into a deserted place. And the crowds were looking for him; and when they reached him, they wanted to prevent him from leaving them.

LUKE 4:42 NRSV

Jesus is so significant, so important, that the world's entire dating system is based on the point in time when He was born on earth. Years are numbered as either b.c. (before Christ) or a.d. (anno Domini, Latin for "in the year of our Lord," or basically, after Jesus' birth).

First and last

This is the message from the one who is the First and the Last, who died and is alive *(the Lord Jesus Christ)*.   REVELATION 2:8 NLT

When I saw him, I fell at his feet as though dead. But he placed his right hand on me, saying, "Do not be afraid; I am the first and the last, and the living one. I was dead, and see, I am alive forever and ever; and I have the keys of Death and of Hades."   REVELATION 1:17–18 NRSV

Firstborn

He is the image of the invisible God, the first-born of all creation. . . . He is before all things.   COLOSSIANS 1:15–17 RSV

When he [God] brings the first-born [Jesus] into the world, he says, "Let all God's angels worship him."   HEBREWS 1:6 RSV

Jesus Christ, the faithful witness, the firstborn of the dead, and the ruler of the kings of the earth. To him who loves us and freed us from our sins by his blood, and made us to be a kingdom, priests serving his God and Father, to him be glory and dominion forever and ever. Amen.   REVELATION 1:5–6 NRSV

Flesh

And the Word [Jesus] became flesh and dwelt among us, full of grace and truth; we have beheld his glory, glory as of the only Son from the Father. JOHN 1:14 RSV

Forgiving

And Jesus said to her, "Neither do I condemn you; go and sin no more." JOHN 8:11 NKJV

But where there was much sin, there was much more grace. ROMANS 5:20 BBE

The greater the sin, the more Christ forgave and covered with His blood.

And be kind to one another, tenderhearted, forgiving one another, even as God in Christ forgave you. EPHESIANS 4:32 NKJV

Bear with one another and, if anyone has a complaint against another, forgive each other; just as the Lord has forgiven you, so you also must forgive. COLOSSIANS 3:13 NRSV

Then Jesus said, "Father, forgive them; for they do not know what they are doing."

LUKE 23:34 NRSV

Even when people nailed Jesus to the cross, cruelly forcing Him into a humiliating and torturous death, Jesus still interceded and prayed for them!

So there is now no condemnation awaiting those who belong to Christ Jesus.   ROMANS 8:1 TLB

Freedom

"You are truly my [Jesus'] disciples if you keep obeying my teachings. And you will know the truth, and the truth will set you free."

JOHN 8:31–32 NLT

Friend

"I [Jesus] do not call you servants any longer, because the servant does not know what the master is doing; but I have called you friends, because I have made known to you everything that I have heard from my Father."   JOHN 15:15 NRSV

"Even now my witness is in heaven; my advocate is on high. My intercessor is my friend as my eyes pour out tears to God; on behalf of a man he pleads with God as a man pleads for his friend." JOB 16:19–21 NIV

There is a friend who sticks closer than a brother. PROVERBS 18:24 NKJV

If we confess our sins, he who is faithful and just will forgive us our sins and cleanse us from all unrighteousness. 1 JOHN 1:9 NRSV

"There are many rooms in my Father's home, and I am going to prepare a place for you. . . . When everything is ready, I will come and get you, so that you will always be with me where I am." JOHN 14:2–3 NLT

Fulfillment

"Do not think that I [Jesus] have come to abolish the law or the prophets; I have come not to abolish but to fulfill. For truly I tell you, until heaven and earth pass away, not one letter, not one stroke of a letter, will pass from the law until all is accomplished."   MATTHEW 5:17–18 NRSV

"The Law and the Prophets" are explained in these two verses:

1. "You shall love the LORD your God with all your heart, with all your soul, and with all your mind. This is the first and great commandment. And the second is like it: You shall love your neighbor as yourself. On these two command- ments hang all the Law and the Prophets."

MATTHEW 22:37–40 NKJV

2. "Therefore, whatever you want men to do to you, do also to them, for this is the Law and the Prophets."   MATTHEW 7:12 NKJV

Do not gloat when your enemy falls; when he stumbles, do not let your heart rejoice, or the LORD will see and disapprove and turn his wrath away from him.   PROVERBS 24:17–18 NIV

Jesus replied, "Let it be so now; it is proper for us to do this to fulfill all righteousness." Then John consented. . . . And a voice from heaven said, "This is my Son, whom I love; with him I am well pleased."   MATTHEW 3:15, 17 NIV

Jesus' actions completely fulfill and magnify God's attributes in an extreme way that no man could have done. In fact, His teachings were unheard of and quite radical at that time. For example (from God's attribute of "Merciful"):

Jesus' words:
"But I say to you, love your enemies, bless those who curse you, do good to those who hate you, and pray for those who spitefully use you and persecute you."   MATTHEW 5:44 NKJV

Jesus' actions:
When they came to the place that is called The Skull, they crucified Jesus there with the criminals, one on his right and one on his left. Then Jesus said, "Father, forgive them; for they do not know what they are doing."   LUKE 23:33–34 NRSV

(See also "Prophecy fulfilled.")

JESUS. . .G

Gate

Jesus told him, "I am the way, the truth, and the life. No one can come to the Father except through me."
JOHN 14:6 NLT

So again Jesus said to them, "Very truly, I tell you, I am the gate for the sheep. . . . I am the gate. Whoever enters by me will be saved, and will come in and go out and find pasture. The thief comes only to steal and kill and destroy. I came that they may have life, and have it abundantly."
JOHN 10:7–10 NRSV

Jesus is the only entrance through which we may have eternal life and a relationship with God. (See "Gospel.")

Generous

Jesus stood and cried, saying, If any man thirst, let him come unto me, and drink. He that believeth on me, as the scripture hath said, out of his belly shall flow rivers of living water.

JOHN 7:37–38 KJV

For you know the generous act of our Lord Jesus Christ, that though he was rich, yet for your sakes he became poor, so that by his poverty you might become rich.

2 CORINTHIANS 8:9 NRSV

God saved you by his special favor when you believed. And you can't take credit for this; it is a gift from God. Salvation is not a reward for the good things we have done, so none of us can boast about it.   EPHESIANS 2:8–9 NLT

Tell them to use their money to do good. They should be rich in good works and should give generously to those in need, always being ready to share with others whatever God has given them.   1 TIMOTHY 6:18 NLT

For by grace you have been saved through faith, and that not of yourselves; it is the gift of God, not of works, lest anyone should boast.

EPHESIANS 2:8–9 NKJV

Gentle

I. . .appeal to you by the meekness and gentleness of Christ.   2 CORINTHIANS 10:1 NRSV

Let your gentle behaviour be clear to all men. The Lord is near.   PHILIPPIANS 4:5 BBE

"Come to me [Jesus], all you that are weary and are carrying heavy burdens, and I will give you rest. Take my yoke upon you, and learn from me; for I am gentle and humble in heart, and you will find rest for your souls. For my yoke is easy, and my burden is light."

MATTHEW 11:28–30 NRSV

"Look, your king is coming to you, humble, and mounted on a donkey."   MATTHEW 21:5 NRSV

The crushed stem will not be broken by him; and the feebly burning light will he not put out, till he has made righteousness overcome all.

MATTHEW 12:20 BBE

"A bruised reed he will not break, and a smoldering wick he will not snuff out. In faithfulness he will bring forth justice." ISAIAH 42:3 NIV

O Jerusalem, Jerusalem, thou that killest the prophets, and stonest them which are sent unto thee, how often would I have gathered thy children together, even as a hen gathereth her chickens under her wings, and ye would not!

MATTHEW 23:37 KJV

Glorious

This, the first of his miraculous signs, Jesus performed in Cana of Galilee. He thus revealed his glory, and his disciples put their faith in him.

JOHN 2:11 NIV

None of the rulers of this age understood this; for if they had, they would not have crucified the Lord of glory. 1 CORINTHIANS 2:8 RSV

And all of us *(who love the Lord Jesus),* with unveiled faces, seeing the glory of the Lord as though reflected in a mirror, are being transformed into the same image from one degree of glory to another; for this comes from the Lord, the Spirit. 2 CORINTHIANS 3:18 NRSV

God

"Listen! The virgin shall conceive a child! She shall give birth to a Son, and he shall be called 'Emmanuel' *(meaning 'God is with us').*"

MATTHEW 1:23 TLB

For in Christ there is all of God in a human body. COLOSSIANS 2:9 TLB

I was shown mercy so that in me, the worst of sinners, Christ Jesus might display his unlimited patience as an example for those who would believe on him and receive eternal life. Now to the King eternal, immortal, invisible, the only God, be honor and glory for ever and ever.

1 TIMOTHY 1:16–17 NIV

For to which of the angels did God ever say, "You are my Son; today I have begotten you"? Or again, "I will be his Father, and he will be my Son"? And again, when he brings the firstborn into the world, he says, "Let all God's angels worship him." HEBREWS 1:5–6, PSALM 2:7, 2 SAMUEL 7:13–16 NRSV

God speaks of his angels as messengers swift as the wind and as servants made of flaming fire; but of his Son he says, "Your Kingdom, O God, will last forever and ever; its commands are always just and right." HEBREWS 1:7–8 TLB

But of the Son he says, . . ."In the beginning, Lord, you founded the earth, and the heavens are the work of your hands; they will perish, but you remain; they will all wear out like clothing; like a cloak you will roll them up, and like clothing they will be changed. But you are the same, and your years will never end." But to which of the angels has he ever said, "Sit at my right hand until I make your enemies a footstool for your feet"? HEBREWS 1:8, 10–13 NRSV

Your throne, O God, is forever and ever; a scepter of righteousness is the scepter of Your kingdom. You love righteousness and hate wickedness; therefore God, Your God, has anointed You with the oil of gladness more than Your companions.

PSALM 45:6–7 NKJV

Good

His divine power has given us everything needed for life and godliness, through the knowledge of him who called us by his own glory and goodness.   2 PETER 1:3 NRSV

Beloved, do not imitate what is evil but imitate what is good. Whoever does good is from God; whoever does evil has not seen God.

3 JOHN 11 NRSV

God's solid foundation stands firm, sealed with this inscription: "The Lord knows those who are his," and, "Everyone who confesses the name of the Lord must turn away from wickedness."

2 TIMOTHY 2:19 NIV

Gospel

Gospel means "good news." Jesus Christ is the "good news." The penalty or consequence for falling short of God's standards is death. Jesus died for our sin penalty in our place, and then conquered death by rising again. We can be saved from our sin penalty by believing on Him, asking Him into our hearts to remove our sins, and allowing Him to be the living Lord of our lives.

By which also ye are saved, if ye keep in memory what I preached unto you, unless ye have believed in vain. For I delivered unto you first of all that which I also received, how that Christ died for our sins according to the scriptures; and that he was buried, and that he rose again the third day according to the scriptures.

1 CORINTHIANS 15:2–4 KJV

And you, who in the past were cut off and at war with God in your minds through evil works, he has now made one in the body of his flesh through death, so that you might be holy and without sin and free from all evil before him: If you keep yourselves safely based in the faith, not moved from the hope of the good news which came to you, and which was given to every living being under heaven; of which I, Paul, was made a servant. COLOSSIANS 1:21–23 BBE

JESUS. . .H

Head

Christ. . .is the head over every power and
authority.   COLOSSIANS 2:10 NIV

God put this power to work in Christ when he
raised him from the dead and seated him at his
right hand in the heavenly places, far above all
rule and authority and power and dominion,
and above every name that is named, not only
in this age but also in the age to come. And he
has put all things under his feet and has made
him the head over all things for the church,
which is his body, the fullness of him who fills
all in all.   EPHESIANS 1:20–23 NRSV

And he is the head of the body, the church: the starting point of all things.

COLOSSIANS 1:18 BBE

For no one ever hates his own body, but he nourishes and tenderly cares for it, just as Christ does for the church, because we are members of his body.

EPHESIANS 5:29–30 NRSV

But speaking the truth in love, we must grow up in every way into him who is the head, into Christ, from whom the whole body, joined and knit together by every ligament with which it is equipped, as each part is working properly, promotes the body's growth in building itself up in love.

EPHESIANS 4:15–16 NRSV

He has lost connection with the Head [Jesus], from whom the whole body, supported and held together by its ligaments and sinews, grows as God causes it to grow. Since you died with Christ to the basic principles of this world, why, as though you still belonged to it, do you submit to its rules?

COLOSSIANS 2:19–20 NIV

Healer

Jesus said to him, "Stand up, take your mat and walk." At once the man was made well, and he took up his mat and began to walk.

JOHN 5:8–9 NRSV

Then great multitudes came to Him, having with them the lame, blind, mute, maimed, and many others; and they laid them down at Jesus' feet, and He healed them. So the multitude marveled when they saw the mute speaking, the maimed made whole, the lame walking, and the blind seeing; and they glorified the God of Israel.

MATTHEW 15:30–31 NKJV

He healed many who were sick with various diseases, and cast out many demons; and He did not allow the demons to speak, because they knew Him.

MARK 1:34 NKJV

But it was for our sins he was wounded, and for our evil doings he was crushed: he took the punishment by which we have peace, and by his wounds we are made well.

ISAIAH 53:5 BBE

And great multitudes followed Him [Jesus], and He healed them all.   MATTHEW 12:15 NKJV

O LORD my God, I cried out to You, and You healed me. O LORD, You brought my soul up from the grave; You have kept me alive, that I should not go down to the pit.

PSALM 30:2–3 NKJV

Heir

Long ago God spoke to our ancestors in many and various ways by the prophets, but in these last days he has spoken to us by a Son, whom he appointed heir of all things, through whom he also created the worlds. He is the reflection of God's glory and the exact imprint of God's very being, and he sustains all things by his powerful word. When he had made purification for sins, he sat down at the right hand of the Majesty on high, having become as much superior to angels as the name he has inherited is more excellent than theirs.   HEBREWS 1:1–4 NRSV

Helper

For since he himself has now been through suffering and temptation, he knows what it is like when we suffer and are tempted, and he is wonderfully able to help us.   HEBREWS 2:18 TLB

We all know that Jesus came to help the descendants of Abraham *(i.e., people),* not to help the angels.   HEBREWS 2:16 NLT

And after you have undergone pain for a little time, the God of all grace who has given you a part in his eternal glory through Christ Jesus, will himself give you strength and support, and make you complete in every good thing.

1 PETER 5:10 BBE

Hero

We are always looking for a hero, someone strong, capable, compassionate, a willing champion for the defenseless. Jesus is the hero among heroes. He gave up His awesome heritage for us. He endured agony, torture and humiliation, to even past the point of

67

dying, for us. But the best part of it is that He has "won over the enemy." He conquered death and is right now alive, victorious, and compassionately helping any who turns to Him. Unlike other heroes, He is available any time we seek Him, and He does not have any ulterior or selfish motives—simply our own eternal good. But He is so gentle and quiet that most people do not know He is there for them—how tragic for them! It is very easy to miss Him when we are busy with our own lives and our own thoughts and our own understanding.

For since he himself has now been through suffering and temptation, he knows what it is like when we suffer and are tempted, and he is wonderfully able to help us.   HEBREWS 2:18 TLB

For you know the grace of our Lord Jesus Christ, that though He was rich, yet for your sakes He became poor, that you through His poverty might become rich.   2 CORINTHIANS 8:9 NKJV

He himself bore our sins in his body on the cross, so that, free from sins, we might live for righteousness; by his wounds you have been healed.

1 PETER 2:24 NRSV

Since the children [us] have flesh and blood, he [Jesus] too shared in their humanity so that by his death he might destroy him who holds the power of death—that is, the devil—and free those who all their lives were held in slavery by their fear of death.　　　HEBREWS 2:14–15 NIV

He was despised and rejected—a man of sorrows, acquainted with bitterest grief. We turned our backs on him and looked the other way when he went by. He was despised, and we did not care. Yet it was our weaknesses he carried; it was our sorrows that weighed him down. And we thought his troubles were a punishment from God for his own sins! But he was wounded and crushed for our sins. He was beaten that we might have peace. He was whipped, and we were healed!　　　ISAIAH 53:3–5 NLT

"You give me your shield of victory, and your right hand sustains me; you stoop down to make me great."　　　PSALM 18:35 NIV

"Christ Jesus died, or rather has risen to life again. He is also at the right hand of God, and is interceding for us."　　　ROMANS 8:34 WEYMOUTHS

Jesus' death pays for our sin penalty (which is our death), if we make Him Lord in our hearts. But more importantly, after we have received Jesus as Lord in our hearts, His resurrection, His being alive this moment, gives us the power this moment (!) to overcome. Through Jesus we can live according to God's righteousness and according to His perfect and pleasing will, instead of the fleeting desires and worries caused by this world.

"He [Jesus] is able to save completely those who come to God through him, because he always lives to intercede *(hit the mark)* for them."

HEBREW 7:25 NIV

If then you have a new life with Christ, give your attention to the things of heaven, where Christ is seated at the right hand of God.

COLOSSIANS 3:1 BBE

High priest
See "Priest."

For this reason, holy brothers, marked out to have a part in heaven, give thought to Jesus the representative and high priest of our faith.

HEBREWS 3:1 BBE

Holy

There was. . .a man with an unclean spirit, and he cried out, "What have you to do with us, Jesus of Nazareth? Have you come to destroy us? I know who you are, the Holy One of God."

MARK 1:23–24 NRSV

For David speaketh concerning him. . . Because thou wilt not leave my [Jesus'] soul in hell, neither wilt thou suffer thine Holy One to see corruption. . . . He seeing this before spake of the resurrection of Christ, that his soul was not left in hell, neither his flesh did see corruption. This Jesus hath God raised up, whereof we all are witnesses.

ACTS 2:25, 27, 31–32 KJV

Therefore my heart is glad and my tongue rejoices; my body also will rest secure, because you will not abandon me to the grave, nor will you let your Holy One see decay. You have made known to me the path of life; you will fill me with joy in your presence, with eternal pleasures at your right hand.

PSALM 16:9–11 NIV

"Just and true are Your ways, O King of the saints! Who shall not fear You, O Lord, and glorify Your name? For You alone are holy."

REVELATION 15:3–4 NKJV

Honored

Let the same mind be in you that was in Christ Jesus, who, though he was in the form of God, did not regard equality with God as something to be exploited, but emptied himself, taking the form of a slave, being born in human likeness. And being found in human form, he humbled himself and became obedient to the point of death—even death on a cross. Therefore God also highly exalted him and gave him the name that is above every name, so that at the name of Jesus every knee should bend, in heaven and on earth and under the earth.

PHILIPPIANS 2:5–10 NRSV

When the Lord Jesus had finished talking with them, he was taken up into heaven and sat down in the place of honor at God's right hand.

MARK 16:19 NLT

But Stephen, full of the Holy Spirit, gazed steadily upward into heaven and saw the glory of God, and he saw Jesus standing in the place of honor at God's right hand. And he told them, "Look, I see the heavens opened and the Son of Man standing in the place of honor at God's right hand!"   ACTS 7:55–56 NLT

Then I heard every creature in heaven and on earth and under the earth and in the sea, and all that is in them, singing, "To the one seated on the throne and to the Lamb be blessing and honor and glory and might forever and ever!"
                    REVELATION 5:13 NRSV

God put this power to work in Christ when he raised him from the dead and seated him at his right hand in the heavenly places, far above all rule and authority and power and dominion, and above every name that is named, not only in this age but also in the age to come. And he has put all things under his feet and has made him the head over all things for the church, which is his body, the fullness of him who fills all in all.   EPHESIANS 1:20–23 NRSV

"But from now on the Son of Man will be seated at the right hand of the power of God."

LUKE 22:69 NRSV

Hope

And he [Jesus] said to them in answer, O generation without faith, how long will I have to be with you? how long will I put up with you? let him come to me.

MARK 9:19 BBE

No case is hopeless with Jesus, who lives even today.

We are troubled on every side, yet not distressed; we are perplexed, but not in despair; persecuted, but not forsaken; cast down, but not destroyed; always bearing about in the body the dying of the Lord Jesus, that the life also of Jesus might be made manifest in our body. . . . For our light affliction, which is but for a moment, worketh for us a far more exceeding and eternal weight of glory; while we look not at the things which are seen, but at the things which are not seen: for the things which are seen are temporal; but the things which are not seen are eternal.

2 CORINTHIANS 4:8–10, 4:17–18 KJV

Waiting for the blessed hope and manifestation of the glory of our great God and Saviour Jesus Christ, who did give himself for us, that he might ransom us from all lawlessness, and might purify to himself a peculiar people, zealous of good works.   TITUS 2:13–14 YLT

For the Lord himself, with a cry of command, with the archangel's call and with the sound of God's trumpet, will descend from heaven, and the dead in Christ will rise first. Then we who are alive, who are left, will be caught up in the clouds together with them to meet the Lord in the air; and so we will be with the Lord forever. Therefore encourage one another with these words.

1 THESSALONIANS 4:16–18 NRSV

Humble
See "Selfless."

Although he [Christ] was abused, he never tried to get even. And when he suffered, he made no threats. Instead, he had faith in God, who judges fairly.   1 PETER 2:23 CEV

For truly the Son of man did not come to have servants, but to be a servant, and to give his life for the salvation of men.   MARK 10:45 BBE

Don't be selfish; don't live to make a good impression on others. Be humble, thinking of others as better than yourself.   PHILIPPIANS 2:3 NLT

Let the same mind be in you that was in Christ Jesus, who, though he was in the form of God, did not regard equality with God as something to be exploited, but emptied himself, taking the form of a slave, being born in human likeness. And being found in human form, he humbled himself and became obedient to the point of death—even death on a cross.

PHILIPPIANS 2:5–8 NRSV

Husband

For this cause will a man go away from his father and mother and be joined to his wife, and the two will become one flesh. This is a great secret: but my words are about Christ and the church.   EPHESIANS 5:31–32 BBE

For as a young man takes a virgin for his wife, so will your maker be married to you: and as a husband has joy in his bride, so will the Lord your God be glad over you.   ISAIAH 62:5 BBE

Come back. . .says the Lord; for I am a husband to you.   JEREMIAH 3:14 BBE

JESUS. . .I

I AM
(Self-existing, self-sufficient)

Jesus said to them, "Most assuredly, I say to you, before Abraham was, I AM." JOHN 8:58 NKJV

Jesus, being one with God, always has existed—and always will.

And he [Jesus] said to them, You are of the earth; I am from heaven: you are of this world; I am not of this world. For this reason I said to you that death will overtake you in your sins: for if you have not faith that I am he, death will come to you while you are in your sins.

JOHN 8:23–24 BBE

And God said to Moses, "I AM WHO I AM."
And He said, "Thus you shall say to the children of Israel, 'I AM has sent me to you.' "

EXODUS 3:14 NKJV

Illuminating
See "Light."

"I [Jesus] am the light of the world."

JOHN 9:5 RSV

Imitator of God the Father

Jesus said to them, "Very truly, I tell you, the Son
can do nothing on his own, but only what he sees
the Father doing; for whatever the Father does,
the Son does likewise." JOHN 5:19 NRSV

And we desire that each one of you show the
same diligence. . .that you do not become slug-
gish, but imitate those who through faith and
patience inherit the promises.

HEBREWS 6:11–12 NKJV

Beloved, do not imitate what is evil, but what is good. He who does good is of God, but he who does evil has not seen God.   3 JOHN 11 NKJV

Remember your leaders, those who spoke the word of God to you; consider the outcome of their way of life, and imitate their faith.

HEBREWS 13:7 NRSV

Immutable

Jesus Christ is the same yesterday, today, and forever.   HEBREWS 13:8 NKJV

Impartial

Then Peter began to speak: "I now realize how true it is that God does not show favoritism but accepts men from every nation who fear him and do what is right."   ACTS 10:34–35 NIV

Indispensable

Jesus explains, I am the vine, you are the branches: he who is in me at all times as I am in him, gives much fruit, because without me you are able to do nothing.　　　　JOHN 15:5 BBE

Innocent

"Even though they found no cause for a sentence of death, they asked Pilate to have him [Jesus] killed."　　　　ACTS 13:28 NRSV

For we have not a high priest who is not able to be touched by the feelings of our feeble flesh; but we have one who has been tested in all points as we ourselves are tested, but without sin.

HEBREWS 4:15 BBE

Intercessor

Jesus prayed, My prayer is for them: my prayer is not for the world, but for those whom you have given to me, because they are yours.

JOHN 17:9 BBE

Who then will condemn us? Will Christ Jesus? No, for he is the one who died for us and was raised to life for us and is sitting at the place of highest honor next to God, pleading for us.

ROMANS 8:34 NLT

Consequently he is able for all time to save those who approach God through him, since he always lives to make intercession for them.

HEBREWS 7:25 NRSV

Intimate

Jesus prayed, That they all may be one; as thou, Father, art in me, and I in thee, that they also may be one in us: that the world may believe that thou hast sent me. And the glory which thou gavest me I have given them; that they may be one, even as we are one: I in them, and thou in me, that they may be made perfect in one; and that the world may know that thou hast sent me, and hast loved them, as thou hast loved me.

JOHN 17:21–23 KJV

God is not just "out there somewhere"; He is in each of us who believes and obeys Jesus.

And now I will be no longer in the world, but they are in the world and I come to you. Holy Father, keep them in your name which you have given to me, so that they may be one even as we are one.   JOHN 17:11 BBE

Jesus promises, "I am with you always, even to the end of the age."   MATTHEW 28:20 NKJV

JESUS. . .J

Judge

In the same way, as the Father gives life to the dead, even so the Son gives life to those to whom he is pleased to give it. The Father is not the judge of men, but he has given all decisions into the hands of the Son; so that all men may give honour to the Son even as they give honour to the Father. He who gives no honour to the Son gives no honour to the Father who sent him.

JOHN 5:21–23 BBE

Jesus explains, "I can do nothing on my own. As I hear, I judge; and my judgment is just, because I seek to do not my own will but the will of him who sent me." JOHN 5:30 NRSV

"For just as the Father has life in himself, so he has granted the Son also to have life in himself; and he has given him authority to execute judgment, because he is the Son of Man. Do not be astonished at this; for the hour is coming when all who are in their graves will hear his voice and will come out—those who have done good, to the resurrection of life, and those who have done evil, to the resurrection of condemnation."

JOHN 5:26–29 NRSV

"When the Son of Man comes in his glory, and all the angels with him, then he will sit on the throne of his glory. All the nations will be gathered before him, and he will separate people one from another as a shepherd separates the sheep from the goats, and he will put the sheep at his right hand and the goats at the left. Then the king will say to those at his right hand, 'Come, you that are blessed by my Father, inherit the kingdom prepared for you from the foundation of the world; for I was hungry and you gave me food, I was thirsty and you gave me something to drink, I was a stranger and you welcomed me, I was naked and you gave me clothing, I was sick and you took care of me, I was in prison and you visited me. . . .' Then he will say to those at his left hand, 'You that are accursed, depart from me into the eternal fire prepared for the devil and his angels; for I was hungry and you gave me no food, I was thirsty and you gave me nothing to drink, I was a stranger and you did not welcome me, naked and you did not give me clothing, sick and in prison and you did not visit me. . . .' And these will go away into eternal punishment, but the righteous into eternal life."

MATTHEW 25:31–46 NRSV

Jesus is so passionate that whatever we do for others, or neglect to do for others, He feels as it being done to Him personally (see "Passionate").

Justifier

"Let it be known to you therefore, my brothers, that through this man [Jesus] forgiveness of sins is proclaimed to you; by this Jesus everyone who believes is set free from all those sins from which you could not be freed by the law of Moses."

ACTS 13:38–39 NRSV

The righteous one, my servant, shall make many righteous, and he shall bear their iniquities.

ISAIAH 53:11 NRSV

Therefore, having been justified by faith, we have peace with God through our Lord Jesus Christ, through whom also we have access by faith into this grace in which we stand, and rejoice in hope of the glory of God.

ROMANS 5:1–2 NKJV

JESUS. . .K

Kind

See "Compassionate" and "Willing."

But then God our Savior showed us his kindness and love. He saved us, not because of the good things we did, but because of his mercy.

TITUS 3:4–5 NLT

Then little children were being brought to him [Jesus] in order that he might lay his hands on them and pray. The disciples spoke sternly to those who brought them; but Jesus said, "Let the little children come to me, and do not stop them; for it is to such as these that the kingdom of heaven belongs." MATTHEW 19:13–14 NRSV

Jesus' disciples explain to their accusers how they healed a man: "If we this day are judged for a good deed done to a helpless man, by what means he has been made well, let it be known to you all, and to all the people of Israel, that by the name of Jesus Christ of Nazareth, whom you crucified, whom God raised from the dead, by Him this man stands here before you whole."

ACTS 4:9–10 NKJV

King of kings
See "Messiah."

The LORD hath made known his salvation: his righteousness hath he openly shewed in the sight of the heathen. He hath remembered his mercy and his truth toward the house of Israel: all the ends of the earth have seen the salvation of our God. Make a joyful noise unto the LORD, all the earth: make a loud noise, and rejoice, and sing praise. Sing unto the LORD with the harp; with the harp, and the voice of a psalm. With trumpets and sound of cornets make a joyful noise before the LORD, the King.   PSALM 98:2–6 KJV

Then I saw heaven opened, and there was a white horse! Its rider is called Faithful and True, and in righteousness he judges and makes war. . . . On his robe and on his thigh he has a name inscribed, "King of kings and Lord of lords."   REVELATION 19:11,16 NRSV

Knowledge

Christ, in whom are hidden all the treasures of wisdom and knowledge.   COLOSSIANS 2:2–3 NKJV

JESUS. . .L

Lamb

John saw Jesus coming toward him, and said, "Behold! The Lamb of God who takes away the sin of the world!"   JOHN 1:29 NKJV

Then I saw between the throne and the four living creatures and among the elders a Lamb standing as if it had been slaughtered. . . . The four living creatures and the twenty-four elders fell before the Lamb. . .You are worthy to take the scroll and to open its seals, for you were slaughtered and by your blood you ransomed for God saints from every tribe and language and people and nation."   REVELATION 5:6–9 NRSV

"Worthy is the Lamb, who was slain, to receive power and wealth and wisdom and strength and honor and glory and praise!"

REVELATION 5:12 NIV

"But they have conquered him [Satan] by the blood of the Lamb [Jesus] and by the word of their testimony." REVELATION 12:11 NRSV

Life

"Most assuredly, I [Jesus] say to you, he who hears My word and believes in Him who sent Me has everlasting life, and shall not come into judgment, but has passed from death into life."

JOHN 5:24 NKJV

"I am the one who raises the dead and gives them life again. Anyone who believes in me, even though he dies like anyone else, shall live again. He is given eternal life for believing in me and shall never perish." JOHN 11:25 TLB

"The thief [Satan] comes only to steal and kill and destroy. I [Jesus] came that they may have life, and have it abundantly." JOHN 10:10 NRSV

"Indeed, just as the Father raises the dead and gives them life, so also the Son gives life to whomever he wishes."   JOHN 5:21 NRSV

"You diligently study the Scriptures because you think that by them you possess eternal life. These are the Scriptures that testify about me [Jesus], yet you refuse to come to me to have life."   JOHN 5:39–40 NIV

Let heaven fill your thoughts; don't spend your time worrying about things down here. You should have as little desire for this world as a dead person does. Your real life is in heaven with Christ and God. And when Christ who is our real life comes back again, you will shine with him and share in all his glories.

COLOSSIANS 3:2–4 TLB

I have been crucified with Christ; it is no longer I who live, but Christ lives in me; and the life which I now live in the flesh I live by faith in the Son of God, who loved me and gave Himself for me.   GALATIANS 2:20 NKJV

Light

The LORD is my light and my salvation.

PSALM 27:1 RSV

Jesus said to the people, "I am the light of the world. If you follow me, you won't be stumbling through the darkness, because you will have the light that leads to life." JOHN 8:12 NLT

Jesus shouted to the crowds, "If you trust me, you are really trusting God. For when you see me, you are seeing the one who sent me. I have come as a Light to shine in this dark world, so that all who put their trust in me will no longer wander in the darkness." JOHN 12:44–46 TLB

Jesus replied, "I will deliver you from the Jewish people, as well as from the Gentiles, to whom I now send you, to open their eyes, in order to turn them from darkness to light, and from the power of Satan to God, that they may receive forgiveness of sins and an inheritance among those who are sanctified by faith in Me."

ACTS 26:17–18 NKJV

What came into existence in him (Jesus) was life, and the life was the light of men. And the light goes on shining in the dark; it is not over-come by the dark.   JOHN 1:4–5 BBE

Lion

But one of the twenty-four elders said to me, "Stop weeping! Look, the Lion of the tribe of Judah, the heir to David's throne, has con-quered. He is worthy to open the scroll and break its seven seals."   REVELATION 5:5 NLT

Jesus is the only one who is able to open the scroll because He is the only one Who is worthy enough to reveal its contents. See "Worthy" below.

Living One

But the fact is that Christ has been raised from the dead. He has become the first of a great harvest of those who will be raised to life again.
                    1 CORINTHIANS 15:20 NLT

When they heard that Jesus was alive and that she had seen him, they did not believe it. Afterward Jesus appeared. . .after the Lord Jesus had spoken to them, he was taken up into heaven and he sat at the right hand of God.

MARK 16:11–12, 19 NIV

"But God raised him from the dead; and for many days he appeared to those who came up with him from Galilee to Jerusalem, and they are now his witnesses to the people."

ACTS 13:30–31 NRSV

"In a little while the world will no longer see me (Jesus), but you will see me; because I live, you also will live."   JOHN 14:19 NRSV

"Do not be afraid; I am the first and the last, and the living one. I was dead, and see, I am alive forever and ever; and I have the keys of Death and of Hades."   REVELATION 1:18 NRSV

For the reward of sin is death; but what God freely gives is eternal life in Jesus Christ our Lord.   ROMANS 6:23 BBE

"Barnabas and I are here to bring you this Good News. God's promise to our ancestors has come true in our own time, in that God raised Jesus. This is what the second psalm is talking about when it says concerning Jesus, 'You are my Son. Today I have become your Father.' "

ACTS 13:32–33 NLT

"The fact that God raised him from the dead, never to decay, is stated in these words: 'I will give you the holy and sure blessings promised to David.' So it is stated elsewhere: 'You will not let your Holy One see decay.' "

ACTS 13:34–35, PSALM 16:10 NIV

Because of this my heart is glad, and my glory is full of joy: while my flesh takes its rest in hope. For you will not let my soul be prisoned in the underworld; you will not let your loved one see the place of death. You will make clear to me the way of life; where you are joy is complete; in your right hand there are pleasures for ever and ever.

PSALM 16:9–11 BBE

Lord of all

"Jesus Christ, who is Lord of all. . ."

ACTS 10:36 NIV

And for this purpose Christ went into death and came back again, that he might be the Lord of the dead and of the living.

ROMANS 14:9 BBE

And on his robe and on his leg is a name, KING OF KINGS, AND LORD OF LORDS.

REVELATION 19:16 BBE

Love

To Him who loved us and washed us from our sins in His own blood. . .   REVELATION 1:5 NKJV

Greater love has no man than this, that a man gives up his life for his friends.

JOHN 15:13 BBE

We have the power of loving, because he first had love for us.   1 JOHN 4:19 BBE

And may you have the power to understand, as all God's people should, how wide, how long, how high, and how deep his love really is. May you experience the love of Christ, though it is so great you will never fully understand it.

EPHESIANS 3:18–19 NLT

Neither death nor life, neither angels nor demons, neither the present nor the future, nor any powers, neither height nor depth, nor anything else in all creation, will be able to separate us from the love of God that is in Christ Jesus our Lord.   ROMANS 8:38–39 NIV

JESUS. . .M

Mediator

Under the old system, the blood of goats and bulls and the ashes of a young cow could cleanse people's bodies from ritual defilement. Just think how much more the blood of Christ will purify our hearts from deeds that lead to death so that we can worship the living God. For by the power of the eternal Spirit, Christ offered himself to God as a perfect sacrifice for our sins. That is why he is the one who mediates the new covenant between God and people, so that all who are invited can receive the eternal inheritance God has promised them. For Christ died to set them free from the penalty of the sins they had committed under that first covenant.

HEBREWS 9:13–15 NLT

For there is one God and one Mediator between God and men, the Man Christ Jesus.

1 TIMOTHY 2:5 NKJV

He [Jesus] is able to save completely those who come to God through him, because he always lives to intercede for them.   HEBREWS 7:25 NIV

Meek

Tell ye the daughter of Sion, Behold, thy King cometh unto thee, meek, and sitting upon an ass, and a colt the foal of an ass.   MATTHEW 21:5 KJV

I myself, Paul, appeal to you by the meekness and gentleness of Christ.

2 CORINTHIANS 10:1 NRSV

Merciful

Peter came to [Jesus] and asked, "Sir, how often should I forgive a brother who sins against me? Seven times?" "No!" Jesus replied, "seventy times seven!"   MATTHEW 18:21–22 TLB

When the people nailed Jesus on the cross, He prayed for them, "Father, forgive them; for they do not know what they are doing."

LUKE 23:34 NRSV

Instead of being angry, vengeful, judging or indifferent, Jesus identified with His adversaries, tormentors, and murderers. He showed His love and mercy even to us when we were still His enemies.

And because the children are flesh and blood, he took a body himself and became like them; so that by his death he might put an end to him who had the power of death, that is to say, the Evil One; and let those who all their lives were in chains because of their fear of death, go free. For, truly, he does not take on the life of angels, but that of the seed of Abraham *(humans).* Because of this it was necessary for him to be made like his brothers in every way, so that he might be a high priest full of mercy and keeping faith in everything to do with God, making offerings for the sins of the people.　　HEBREWS 2:14–17 BBE

Messiah
See "King."

"We have found the Messiah" *(which is translated, the Christ).* JOHN 1:41 NKJV

Messiah means Ruler.

"David was looking far into the future and predicting the Messiah's resurrection, and saying that the Messiah's soul would not be left in hell and his body would not decay. He was speaking of Jesus, and we all are witnesses that Jesus rose from the dead. And now he sits on the throne of highest honor in heaven, next to God. And just as promised, the Father gave him the authority to send the Holy Spirit—with the results you are seeing and hearing today. *(No, David was not speaking of himself in these words of his I have quoted)* for he never ascended into the skies. Moreover, he further stated, 'God spoke to my Lord, the Messiah, and said to him, Sit here in honor beside me until I bring your enemies into complete subjection.' Therefore I clearly state to everyone in Israel that God has made this Jesus you crucified to be the Lord, the Messiah!"

ACTS 2:31–36 TLB

The woman said to him, I am certain that the Messiah, who is named Christ, is coming; when he comes he will make all things clear to us.

JOHN 4:25 BBE

Mighty God

For unto us a Child is born, unto us a Son is given; and the government will be upon His shoulder. And His name will be called Wonderful, Counselor, Mighty God, Everlasting Father, Prince of Peace.

ISAIAH 9:6 NKJV

Miraculous

Jesus went throughout Galilee, teaching in their synagogues and proclaiming the good news of the kingdom and curing every disease and every sickness among the people. So his fame spread throughout all Syria, and they brought to him all the sick, those who were afflicted with various diseases and pains, demoniacs, epileptics, and paralytics, and he cured them.

MATTHEW 4:23–24 NRSV

"Go back and report what you have seen and heard: The blind receive sight, the lame walk, those who have leprosy are cured, the deaf hear, the dead are raised, and the good news is preached to the poor."   LUKE 7:22 NIV

And they were filled with great awe and said to one another, "Who then is this, that even the wind and the sea obey him?"   MARK 4:41 NRSV

"Men of Israel, listen to this: Jesus of Nazareth was a man accredited by God to you by miracles, wonders and signs, which God did among you through him, as you yourselves know."

          ACTS 2:22 NIV

"It is by the name of Jesus Christ of Nazareth, whom you crucified but whom God raised from the dead, that this man stands before you healed."   ACTS 4:10 NIV

Jesus did many other miraculous signs in the presence of his disciples, which are not recorded in this book.   JOHN 20:30 NIV

But He [Jesus] said, "The things which are impossible with men are possible with God."

LUKE 18:27 NKJV

Morning Star

"I, Jesus. . .am. . .the Bright and Morning Star."

REVELATION 22:16 NKJV

JESUS. . .N

Near

Seek the LORD while He may be found, call upon Him while He is near.   ISAIAH 55:6 NKJV

"Look, the virgin shall conceive and bear a son [Jesus], and they shall name him Emmanuel," which means, "God is with us."

MATTHEW 1:23 NRSV

Nuturing

"Do not rejoice at this, that the spirits submit to you, but rejoice that your names are written in heaven."   LUKE 10:20 NRSV

Our relationship with Jesus is much more important than what we are able to do through Him.

Jesus. . .O

Obedient

Jesus prayed, "Father, if you are willing, please take this cup of suffering (his coming ordeal and crucifixion on the cross) away from me. Yet I want your will, not mine."   LUKE 22:42 NLT

Jesus' human need was opposite of God the Father's will. Jesus' need to avoid the torture and humiliation on the cross was so great that He had to pray this prayer multiple times, each time more earnestly, that His Father's will be done instead of His.

"And being in anguish, he prayed more earnestly."
LUKE 22:44 NIV

"For I have come down from heaven, not to do My own will, but the will of Him who sent Me."

JOHN 6:38 NKJV

"I have glorified You on the earth. I have finished the work which You have given Me to do."

JOHN 17:4 NKJV

"If you keep My commandments, you will abide in My love, just as I have kept My Father's commandments and abide in His love."

JOHN 15:10 NKJV

Though Jesus is God, when He was the Son of Man, He was obedient to His human parents.

Then he went down with them and came to Nazareth, and was obedient to them. LUKE 2:51 NRSV

John the Baptist did not want to baptize Jesus, because he recognized that Jesus, as the Son of God, was greater than John was. But Jesus did not use His superior position as an excuse to be disobedient.

But Jesus answered him, "Let it be so now; for it is proper for us in this way to fulfill all righteousness." Then he consented *(to baptize Jesus)*. . . .

And a voice from heaven said, "This is my Son, the Beloved, with whom I am well pleased."

MATTHEW 3:15, 17 NRSV

Christ Jesus, who, though he was in the form of God, did not regard equality with God as something to be exploited, but emptied himself, taking the form of a slave, being born in human likeness. And being found in human form, he humbled himself and became obedient to the point of death—even death on a cross.

PHILIPPIANS 2:6–8 NRSV

Omega

Look! He comes with the clouds of heaven. And everyone will see him—even those who pierced him. And all the nations of the earth will weep because of him. Yes! Amen! "I am the Alpha and the Omega—the beginning and the end," says the Lord God. "I am the one who is, who always was, and who is still to come, the Almighty One."

REVELATION 1:7–8 NLT

One and Only

The Word became flesh and made his dwelling among us. We have seen his glory, the glory of the One and Only, who came from the Father, full of grace and truth.   JOHN 1:14 NIV

Organized

And Jesus made them all be seated in groups on the green grass. And they were placed in groups, by hundreds and by fifties.   MARK 6:39–40 BBE

Even though Jesus miraculously provided enough fish and loaves of bread for five thousand people, He maintained order. He divided the huge number of people into smaller, manageable sized groups.

Then [Jesus] said to them, Give to Caesar the things which are Caesar's, and to God the things which are God's.   MATTHEW 22:21 BBE

God is not one who likes things to be disorderly and upset. He likes harmony.

1 CORINTHIANS 14:33 TLB

Overcomer

Jesus explains, I have said all these things to you so that in me you may have peace. In the world you have trouble: but take heart! I have overcome the world.　　　　JOHN 16:33 BBE

He who is in you [Jesus] is greater than he who is in the world [Satan].　　　　1 JOHN 4:4 NKJV

Do not be overcome by evil, but overcome evil with good.　　　　ROMANS 12:21 RSV

For loving God is keeping his laws: and his laws are not hard. Anything which comes from God is able to overcome the world: and the power by which we have overcome the world is our faith. Who is able to overcome the world but the man who has faith that Jesus is the Son of God?

　　　　1 JOHN 5:3–5 BBE

Together they will wage war against the Lamb [Jesus], and the Lamb will conquer them; for he is Lord over all lords, and King of kings, and his people are the called and chosen and faithful ones.　　　　REVELATION 17:14 TLB

"He who overcomes shall not be hurt by the second death."   REVELATION 2:11 NKJV

They defeated him [Satan] by the blood of the Lamb [Jesus] and by their testimony; for they did not love their lives but laid them down for him.
                    REVELATION 12:11 TLB

"To him who overcomes I [Jesus] will grant to sit with Me on My throne, as I also overcame and sat down with My Father on His throne."
                    REVELATION 3:21 NKJV

JESUS. . .P

Partner

And the disciples went everywhere and preached, and the Lord worked with them, confirming what they said by many miraculous signs.

MARK 16:20 NLT

Passionate

(I pray) that Christ may dwell in your hearts by faith; that ye, being rooted and grounded in love, may be able to comprehend with all saints what is the breadth, and length, and depth, and height; and to know the love of Christ, which passeth knowledge, that ye might be filled with all the fulness of God.　EPHESIANS 3:17–19 KJV

"I [Jesus] know your works, that you are neither cold nor hot. I could wish you were cold or hot. So then, because you are lukewarm, and neither cold nor hot, I will vomit you out of My mouth."

REVELATION 3:15–16 NKJV

Patient

But that is why God had mercy on me, so that Christ Jesus could use me as a prime example of his great patience with even the worst sinners. Then others will realize that they, too, can believe in him and receive eternal life.

1 TIMOTHY 1:16 NLT

Peace

For he [Jesus] is our peace; in his flesh he has made both groups into one and has broken down the dividing wall, that is, the hostility between us.

EPHESIANS 2:14 NRSV

The LORD is Peace.

JUDGES 6:24 NKJV

Jesus instructs, "I give you peace, the kind of peace that only I can give. It isn't like the peace that this world can give. So don't be worried or afraid." JOHN 14:27 CEV

Do not be anxious about anything, but in everything, by prayer and petition, with thanksgiving, present your requests to God. And the peace of God, which transcends all understanding, will guard your hearts and your minds in Christ Jesus. PHILIPPIANS 4:6–7 NIV

Do you want more and more of God's kindness and peace? Then learn to know him better and better. 2 PETER 1:2 TLB

And His name will be called Wonderful, Counselor, Mighty God, Everlasting Father, Prince of Peace. Of the increase of His government and peace there will be no end. ISAIAH 9:6–7 NKJV

Perfect

The precious blood of Christ, like that of a lamb without defect or blemish.

1 PETER 1:19 NRSV

Having then a great high priest, who has made his way through the heavens, even Jesus the Son of God, let us be strong in our faith. For we have not a high priest who is not able to be touched by the feelings of our feeble flesh; but we have one who has been tested in all points as we ourselves are tested, but without sin.

HEBREWS 4:14–15 BBE

And this is my prayer, that your love may overflow more and more with knowledge and full insight to help you to determine what is best, so that in the day of Christ you may be pure and blameless, having produced the harvest of righteousness that comes through Jesus Christ for the glory and praise of God.

PHILIPPIANS 1:9–11 NRSV

Permanent

God took an oath that Christ would always be a priest, but he never did this for any other priest. Only to Jesus did he say, "The Lord has taken an oath and will not break his vow: 'You are a priest forever.'" HEBREWS 7:20–21 NLT

Also there were many priests, because they were prevented by death from continuing. But He, because He continues forever, has an unchangeable priesthood.

HEBREWS 7:23–24 NKJV

Personal

"He calls his own. . .by name."

JOHN 10:3 NRSV

See "Passionate."

Power

I can do all things through Christ who strengthens me. PHILIPPIANS 4:13 NKJV

And the seventy came back with joy, saying, Lord [Jesus], even the evil spirits are under our power in your name. LUKE 10:17 BBE

The Kingdom of God is not just talking; it is living by God's power. 1 CORINTHIANS 4:20 TLB

God put this power to work in Christ when he raised him from the dead and seated him at his right hand in the heavenly places, far above all rule and authority and power and dominion, and above every name that is named, not only in this age but also in the age to come.

EPHESIANS 1:20–21 NRSV

And he [God] has put all things under his [Jesus'] feet and has made him the head over all things for the church, which is his body, the fullness of him who fills all in all.

EPHESIANS 1:22–23 NRSV

And Jesus came and spoke to them, saying, "All authority has been given to Me in heaven and on earth." MATTHEW 28:18 NKJV

Jesus said to His followers, "See, I have given you authority to tread on snakes and scorpions, and over all the power of the enemy; and nothing will hurt you." LUKE 10:19 NRSV

"For as the lightning comes from the east and flashes as far as the west, so will be the coming of the Son of Man." MATTHEW 24:27 NRSV

Christ's first coming to earth was miraculous but humble through the virgin birth. Christ's second coming to earth will also be miraculous, but opposite in the display and use of His power. His first coming as a baby was to be near us, gently wooing us from evil and the jaws of distress. His second coming will be as King to pronounce uncompromising judgment, compelling justice. Seek the Lord while He is near!

For I am not ashamed of the gospel of Christ, for it is the power of God to salvation for everyone who believes, for the Jew first and also for the Greek.   ROMANS 1:16 NKJV

To him who is able to keep you from falling and to present you before his glorious presence without fault and with great joy—to the only God our Savior be glory, majesty, power and authority, through Jesus Christ our Lord, before all ages, now and forevermore! Amen.

JUDE 24–25 NIV

Prayerful

Now in the morning, having risen a long while before daylight, He went out and departed to a solitary place; and there He prayed.

MARK 1:35 NKJV

But now more than ever the word about Jesus spread abroad; many crowds would gather to hear him and to be cured of their diseases. But he would withdraw to deserted places and pray.

LUKE 5:15–16 NRSV

Now during those days he went out to the mountain to pray; and he spent the night in prayer to God.

LUKE 6:12 NRSV

Some of us "Christians" find it an effort to pray five minutes each day, let alone one hour, much less an entire night!

Then Jesus came with them to a place called Gethsemane *(where He knew He would be facing torture and crucifixion),* and said to the disciples, "Sit here while I go and pray over there."

MATTHEW 26:36 NKJV

And when He had sent them away, He departed
to the mountain to pray.   MARK 6:46 NKJV

Precious

For you know that God paid a ransom to save
you from the empty life you inherited from
your ancestors. And the ransom he paid was not
mere gold or silver. He paid for you with the
precious lifeblood of Christ, the sinless, spotless
Lamb of God.   1 PETER 1:18–19 NLT

Therefore, to you who believe, He is precious.
          1 PETER 2:7 NKJV

Then He turned to His disciples and said pri-
vately, "Blessed are the eyes which see the things
you see; for I tell you that many prophets and
kings have desired to see what you see, and have
not seen it, and to hear what you hear, and have
not heard it."   LUKE 10:23–24 NKJV

Priest

Having then a great high priest, who has made his way through the heavens, even Jesus the Son of God, let us be strong in our faith. For we have not a high priest who is not able to be touched by the feelings of our feeble flesh; but we have one who has been tested in all points as we ourselves are tested, but without sin. Then let us come near to the seat of grace without fear, so that mercy may be given to us, and we may get grace for our help in time of need.   HEBREWS 4:14–16 BBE

And so, dear brothers, now we may walk right into the very Holy of Holies, where God is, because of the blood of Jesus. This is the fresh, new, life-giving way that Christ has opened up for us by tearing the curtain—his human body—to let us into the holy presence of God. And since this great High Priest of ours rules over God's household, let us go right in to God himself, with true hearts fully trusting him to receive us because we have been sprinkled with Christ's blood to make us clean and because our bodies have been washed with pure water.   HEBREWS 10:19–22 TLB

Because Jesus lives forever, he has a permanent priesthood. Therefore he is able to save completely those who come to God through him, because he always lives to intercede for them.

HEBREWS 7:24–25NIV

For such a High Priest was fitting for us, who is holy, harmless, undefiled, separate from sinners, and has become higher than the heavens.

HEBREWS 7:26 NKJV

Prince

"The God of our fathers raised Jesus from the dead—whom you had killed by hanging him on a tree. God exalted him to his own right hand as Prince and Savior that he might give repentance and forgiveness of sins."   ACTS 5:30–31 NIV

For a child has been born for us, a son given to us; authority rests upon his shoulders; and he is named Wonderful Counselor, Mighty God, Everlasting Father, Prince of Peace.

ISAIAH 9:6–7 NRSV

Prince of princes. . .   DANIEL 8:25 NKJV

Prophecy fulfilled

Some prophets told how kind God would be to you, and they searched hard to find out more about the way you would be saved. The Spirit of Christ was in them and was telling them how Christ would suffer and would then be given great honor. So they searched to find out exactly who Christ would be and when this would happen.   1 PETER 1:10–11 CEV

Prophet

About the middle of the festival Jesus went up into the temple and began to teach. The Jews were astonished at it, saying, "How does this man have such learning, when he has never been taught?" Then Jesus answered them, "My teaching is not mine but his who sent me. Anyone who resolves to do the will of God will know whether the teaching is from God or whether I am speaking on my own."   JOHN 7:14–17 NRSV

When they heard these words, some in the crowd said, "This is really the prophet."

JOHN 7:40 NRSV

"Jesus of Nazareth, who was a Prophet mighty in deed and word before God and all the people. . . ."

LUKE 24:19 NKJV

Provider

Then he said to me, "It is done! I am the Alpha and the Omega, the beginning and the end. To the thirsty I will give water as a gift from the spring of the water of life."

REVELATION 21:6 NRSV

Purifier

But if we walk in the light, as he is in the light, we have fellowship with one another, and the blood of Jesus, his Son, purifies us from all sin.

1 JOHN 1:7 NIV

Purposeful

I [Jesus] have no desire to do what is pleasing to myself, but only what is pleasing to him who sent me.   JOHN 5:30 BBE

Jesus said to them, "My food is to do the will of Him who sent Me, and to finish His work.
                                        JOHN 4:34 NKJV

"It is not my Father's will that even one of these little ones should perish."   MATTHEW 18:14 TLB

The Lord desires everyone to have eternal life with Him.

JESUS. . .Q

Quiet

His coming will not be with fighting or loud cries; and his voice will not be lifted up in the streets. The crushed stem will not be broken by him; and the feebly burning light will he not put out, till he has made righteousness overcome all. MATTHEW 12:19–20 BBE

JESUS. . .R

Radiant

I saw one like the Son of Man, clothed with a long robe and with a golden sash across his chest. His head and his hair were white as white wool, white as snow; his eyes were like a flame of fire, his feet were like burnished bronze, refined as in a furnace, and his voice was like the sound of many waters. In his right hand he held seven stars, and from his mouth came a sharp, two-edged sword, and his face was like the sun shining with full force.   REVELATION 1:13–16 NRSV

"At midday, . . .along the road I saw a light from heaven, brighter than the sun, shining around me and those who journeyed with me. . . . And He said, 'I am Jesus.' "   ACTS 26:13, 15 NKJV

The Son [Jesus] is the radiance of God's glory and the exact representation of his being, sustaining all things by his powerful word. After he had provided purification for sins, he sat down at the right hand of the Majesty in heaven.

HEBREWS 1:3 NIV

Redeemer

"For I know that my Redeemer lives, and that at the last he will stand upon the earth."

JOB 19:25 NRSV

In Him [Jesus] we have redemption through his blood, the forgiveness of sins, in accordance with the riches of God's grace that he lavished on us with all wisdom and understanding.

EPHESIANS 1:7–8 NIV

Giving thanks to the Father, who has enabled you to share in the inheritance of the saints in the light. He has rescued us from the power of darkness and transferred us into the kingdom of his beloved Son, in whom we have redemption, the forgiveness of sins. COLOSSIANS 1:12–14 NRSV

Rejected

He was in the world, and the world came into being through him; yet the world did not know him. He came to what was his own, and his own people did not accept him. JOHN 1:10–11 NRSV

Then he began to teach them that the Son of Man must undergo great suffering, and be rejected by the elders, the chief priests, and the scribes, and be killed, and after three days rise again. MARK 8:31 NRSV

"But first He must suffer many things and be rejected by this generation." LUKE 17:25 NKJV

In many of the Psalms, David (the shepherd boy who became king of Israel) prophetically describes events and feelings that Jesus would undergo. This psalm describes Jesus after He was arrested in the Garden of Gethsemene. Jesus was scorned, ridiculed and tortured, and He became so bruised and disfigured that people would cringe and flee from seeing such horror and pain. But they still demanded that He be crucified.

Be gracious to me, O LORD, for I am in distress; my eye wastes away from grief, my soul and body also. For my life is spent with sorrow, and my years with sighing; my strength fails because of my misery, and my bones waste away. I am the scorn of all my adversaries, a horror to my neighbors, an object of dread to my acquaintances; those who see me in the street flee from me. I have passed out of mind like one who is dead; I have become like a broken vessel. For I hear the whispering of many—terror all around!—as they scheme together against me, as they plot to take my life.   PSALM 31:9–13 NRSV

Rescuer

How you turned away from idols to serve the true and living God. And they speak of how you are looking forward to the coming of God's Son from heaven—Jesus, whom God raised from the dead. He is the one who has rescued us from the terrors of the coming judgment.

1 THESSALONIANS 1:9–10 NLT

Responsive

And behold, a leper came and worshiped Him, saying, "Lord, if You are willing, You can make me clean." Then Jesus put out His hand and touched him, saying, "I am willing; be cleansed." Immediately his leprosy was cleansed.

MATTHEW 8:2–3 NKJV

But when he saw that the wind was boisterous, he was afraid; and beginning to sink he cried out, saying, "Lord, save me!" And immediately Jesus stretched out His hand and caught him.

MATTHEW 14:30–31 NKJV

Resurrection

Jesus said to her, "I am the resurrection and the life. He who believes in Me, though he may die, he shall live."

JOHN 11:25 NKJV

Peter and John were claiming, on the authority of Jesus, that there is a resurrection of the dead.

ACTS 4:2 NLT

Praise be to the God and Father of our Lord Jesus Christ, who through his great mercy has given us a new birth and a living hope by the coming again of Jesus Christ from the dead, and a heritage fair, holy and for ever new, waiting in heaven for you.   1 PETER 1:3–4 BBE

Revealer

So be careful not to jump to conclusions before the Lord returns as to whether or not someone is faithful. When the Lord comes, he will bring our deepest secrets to light and will reveal our private motives. And then God will give to everyone whatever praise is due.   1 CORINTHIANS 4:5 NLT

No one has ever seen God. It is God the only Son, who is close to the Father's heart, who has made him known.   JOHN 1:18 NRSV

Rewarder

"And behold, I [Jesus] am coming quickly, and My reward is with Me, to give to every one according to his work."   REVELATION 22:12 NKJV

"Blessed are those slaves whom the master finds alert when he comes; truly I tell you, he will fasten his belt and have them sit down to eat, and he will come and serve them. If he comes during the middle of the night, or near dawn, and finds them so, blessed are those slaves."

LUKE 12:37–38 NRSV

Therefore, my beloved brethren, be steadfast, immovable, always abounding in the work of the Lord, knowing that your labor is not in vain in the Lord.   1 CORINTHIANS 15:58 NKJV

So let us not grow weary in doing what is right, for we will reap at harvest-time, if we do not give up.   GALATIANS 6:9 NRSV

Righteous

And he will not be guided in his judging by what he sees, or give decisions by the hearing of his ears: but he will do right in the cause of the poor, and give wise decisions for those in the land who are in need; and the rod of his mouth will come down on the cruel, and with the breath of his lips he will put an end to the evil-doer. And righteousness will be the cord of his robe, and good faith the band round his breast.

ISAIAH 11:3–5 BBE

He shall judge thy people with righteousness, and thy poor with judgment. The mountains shall bring peace to the people, and the little hills, by righteousness. He shall judge the poor of the people, he shall save the children of the needy, and shall break in pieces the oppressor. . . . In his days shall the righteous flourish; and abundance of peace so long as the moon endureth.

PSALM 72:2–4, 7 KJV

Which the Lord, the righteous Judge, will award to me on that day—and not only to me, but also to all who have longed for his appearing.

2 TIMOTHY 4:8 NIV

This is His name by which He will be called: THE LORD OUR RIGHTEOUSNESS.

JEREMIAH 23:6 NKJV

But of the Son he says, Your seat of power, O God, is for ever and ever; and the rod of your kingdom is a rod of righteousness. You have been a lover of righteousness and a hater of evil; and so God, your God, has put the oil of joy on your head more than on the heads of those who are with you.   HEBREWS 1:8–9, PSALM 45:6–7 BBE

Rising Sun

"Because of the tender mercy of our God, by which the rising sun will come to us from heaven to shine on those living in darkness and in the shadow of death, to guide our feet into the path of peace."   LUKE 1:78–79 NIV

Root of David

As you therefore have received Christ Jesus the Lord, so walk in Him, rooted and built up in Him.   COLOSSIANS 2:6–7 NKJV

"I, Jesus, have sent My angel to testify to you these things in the churches. I am the Root and the Offspring of David, the Bright and Morning Star."   REVELATION 22:16 NKJV

And again, Isaiah says, "The Root of Jesse will spring up, one who will arise to rule over the nations; the Gentiles will hope in him."

ROMANS 15:12 NIV

And in that day there shall be a Root of Jesse, Who shall stand as a banner to the people; for the Gentiles shall seek Him, and His resting place shall be glorious.   ISAIAH 11:10 NKJV

And one of the rulers said to me, Do not be sad: see, the Lion of the tribe of Judah, the Root of David, has overcome, and has power to undo the book and its seven stamps.   REVELATION 5:5 BBE

Ruler

"And you, Bethlehem, in the land of Judah, are by no means least among the rulers of Judah; for from you shall come a ruler who is to shepherd my people Israel."   MATTHEW 2:6 NRSV

JESUS. . .S

Sacrifice

"And as Moses lifted up the serpent in the wilderness, even so must the Son of Man be lifted up, that whoever believes in Him should not perish but have eternal life." JOHN 3:14–15 NKJV

"The Son of Man must be lifted up" means that Jesus had to be lifted up on the cross and suspended between heaven and earth; He had to be crucified. When Moses was leading the Israelites through the desert and many people were dying from poisonous snakebites, they could be saved by looking to the snake which was lifted up on Moses' staff (still today's medical symbol!). Now, everyone who looks to Jesus on the cross, where He took our sins onto Himself, is saved and will not die. Jesus had to be sacrificed for

*our sins in order to pay our sin penalty, to make it
possible for us to have eternal life.*

And he [Jesus] took bread, gave thanks and broke
it, and gave it to them, saying, "This is my body
given for you; do this in remembrance of me."
In the same way, after the supper he took the
cup, saying, "This cup is the new covenant in my
blood, which is poured out for you."

LUKE 22:19–20 NIV

So then, my brothers, being able to go into the
holy place without fear, because of the blood of
Jesus, by the new and living way which he made
open for us through the veil, that is to say, his
flesh. . .   HEBREWS 10:19–20 BBE

Christ carried the burden of our sins. He was
nailed to the cross, so that we would stop sinning
and start living right. By his cuts and bruises you
are healed.   1 PETER 2:24 CEV

"I tell you the truth, unless a kernel of wheat falls
to the ground and dies, it remains only a single
seed. But if it dies, it produces many seeds."

JOHN 12:24 NIV

"And from Jesus Christ, the faithful witness, the firstborn from the dead, and the ruler over the kings of the earth. To Him who loved us and washed us from our sins in His own blood."

REVELATION 1:5 NKJV

"Because by one sacrifice he [Jesus] has made perfect forever those who are being made holy."

HEBREWS 10:14 NIV

Satisfier

Jesus replied, "I am the Bread of Life. No one coming to me will ever be hungry again. Those believing in me will never thirst."

JOHN 6:35 TLB

"Do not labor for the food which perishes, but for the food which endures to eternal life, which the Son of man will give to you."

JOHN 6:27 RSV

The Lord says, "I am your. . .exceedingly great reward."   GENESIS 15:1 NKJV

See "Sufficient."

Savior

"For God did not send His Son into the world to condemn the world, but that the world through Him might be saved." JOHN 3:17 NKJV

"For the Son of man came to seek and to save the lost." LUKE 19:10 RSV

"That which is conceived in [Mary] is of the Holy Spirit. And she will bring forth a Son, and you shall call His name JESUS, for He will save His people from their sins."

MATTHEW 1:20–21 NKJV

And, lo, the angel of the Lord came upon them, and the glory of the Lord shone round about them: and they were sore afraid. And the angel said unto them, Fear not: for, behold, I bring you good tidings of great joy, which shall be to all people. For unto you is born this day in the city of David a Saviour, which is Christ the Lord.

LUKE 2:9–11 KJV

Christ is the head of the church *(us who believe Him)*, his body, and is himself its Savior.

EPHESIANS 5:23 RSV

Jesus clarifies, "And if anyone hears My words and does not believe, I do not judge him; for I did not come to judge the world but to save the world."

JOHN 12:47 NKJV

Jesus' first coming to the world was to save anyone who is willing to listen and to follow Him. His future second coming will be to judge.

Paul declares, How true it is, and how I long that everyone should know it, that Christ Jesus came into the world to save sinners—and I was the greatest of them all.   1 TIMOTHY 1:15 TLB

Our Savior Christ Jesus, who abolished *(destroyed)* death and brought life and immortality to light through the gospel.

2 TIMOTHY 1:10 RSV

Jesus assures, "And I give them eternal life, and they shall never perish; neither shall anyone snatch them out of My hand. My Father, who has given them to Me, is greater than all; and no one is able to snatch them out of My Father's hand."   JOHN 10:28–29 NKJV

Selfless

"I do not seek My own will but the will of the Father who sent Me." JOHN 5:30 NKJV

"For I have come down from heaven, not to do My own will, but the will of Him who sent Me." JOHN 6:38 NKJV

Jesus prayed, "Father, if you are willing, please take this cup of suffering *(the impending arrest, torture, and crucifixion)* away from me. Yet I want your will, not mine." LUKE 22:42 NLT

Christ gave his life for evil-doers. Now it is hard for anyone to give his life even for an upright man, though it might be that for a good man someone would give his life. But God has made clear his love to us, in that, when we were still sinners, Christ gave his life for us.

ROMANS 5:6–8 BBE

Jesus not only gave up His life for our sakes, but He even gave up His most precious and intimate relationship with God, His beloved Father.

Jesus cried out with a loud voice, saying, . . . "My God, My God, why have You forsaken Me?"

MATTHEW 27:46 NKJV

When Jesus as the man was crucified, and He took on all our sins and the sins of everyone in the world, God the Father withdrew from Him because of the presence of sin.

See "Humble."

Servant

Jesus taught, "So if I, your Lord and Teacher, have washed your feet, you also ought to wash one another's feet." JOHN 13:14 NRSV

The Lord God declares, My righteous Servant shall justify many, for He shall bear their iniquities *(sins).* Therefore I will divide Him a portion with the great, and He shall divide the spoil with the strong, because He poured out His soul unto death, and He was numbered with the transgressors, and He bore the sin of many, and made intercession for the transgressors.

ISAIAH 53:11–12 NKJV

For truly the Son of man did not come to have servants, but to be a servant, and to give his life for the salvation of men.   MARK 10:45 BBE

Shepherd

He himself bore our sins in his body on the cross, so that, free from sins, we might live for righteousness; by his wounds you have been healed. For you were going astray like sheep, but now you have returned to the shepherd and guardian of your souls.   1 PETER 2:24–25 NRSV

May the God of peace, who through the blood of the eternal covenant brought back from the dead our Lord Jesus, that great Shepherd of the sheep, equip you with everything good for doing his will.   HEBREWS 13:20–21 NIV

For thus says the Lord GOD: "Indeed I Myself will search for My sheep and seek them out. As a shepherd seeks out his flock on the day he is among his scattered sheep, so will I seek out My sheep and deliver them from all the places."   EZEKIEL 34:11–12 NKJV

"I [Jesus] am the good shepherd. The good shepherd lays down his life for the sheep."

JOHN 10:11 RSV

"For the Lamb who is in the midst of the throne will shepherd them and lead them to living fountains of waters. And God will wipe away every tear from their eyes." REVELATION 7:17 NKJV

Sinless

For we do not have a High Priest [Jesus] who cannot sympathize with our weaknesses, but was in all points tempted as we are, yet without sin.

HEBREWS 4:15 NKJV

Son of God

And the angel in answer said to her *(the virgin Mary)*, The Holy Spirit will come on you, and the power of the Most High will come to rest on you, and so that which will come to birth will be named holy, Son of God. LUKE 1:35 BBE

The high priest questioning him said, Are you the Christ, the son of the Holy One? And Jesus said, I am.   MARK 14:61–62 BBE

The man possessed by demons cried out with a loud voice, "What have you to do with me, Jesus, Son of the Most High God?"   MARK 5:7 RSV

And the unclean spirits, whenever they saw Him, fell down before Him and cried out, saying, "You are the Son of God."   MARK 3:11 NKJV

But of the Son he says, "Your throne, O God, is forever and ever, and the righteous scepter is the scepter of your kingdom. You have loved righteousness and hated wickedness."

HEBREWS 1:8–9 NRSV

Son of Man

"For the Son of Man came not to be served but to serve, and to give his life a ransom for many."

MARK 10:45 NRSV

"Hereafter you will see the Son of man seated at the right hand of Power, and coming on the clouds of heaven."   MATTHEW 26:64 RSV

"This Good News was promised long ago by God's prophets in the Old Testament. It is the Good News about his Son, Jesus Christ our Lord, who came as a human baby, born into King David's royal family line; and by being raised from the dead he was proved to be the mighty Son of God, with the holy nature of God himself."   ROMANS 1:2–4 TLB

Jesus is both the Son of God and the Son of Man (descendant of David).

Strength

The LORD is my light and my salvation; whom shall I fear? The LORD is the strength of my life; of whom shall I be afraid?

PSALM 27:1 NKJV

See "Power."

Submissive
See "Obedient."

So Jesus made answer and said, Truly I say to you, The Son is not able to do anything himself; he is able to do only what he sees the Father doing; whatever the Father does the Son does it in the same way.   JOHN 5:19 BBE

"For these are not my own ideas, but I have told you what the Father said to tell you. And I know his instructions lead to eternal life; so whatever he tells me to say, I say!"   JOHN 12:49–50 TLB

Jesus said to them, Truly, you will take of my cup: but to be seated at my right hand and at my left is not for me to give, but it is for those for whom my Father has made it ready.

MATTHEW 20:23 BBE

Yet while Christ was here on earth he pleaded with God, praying with tears and agony of soul to the only one who would save him from [premature] death. And God heard his prayers because of his strong desire to obey God at all times.

HEBREWS 5:7 TLB

He [Jesus] was heard because of his reverent submission. HEBREWS 5:7 NRSV

Jesus knew he would be crucified: "Now is my soul troubled. And what shall I say? 'Father, save me from this hour'? No, for this purpose I have come to this hour." JOHN 12:27 RSV

Suffering

"For as the lightning flashes and lights up the sky from one side to the other, so will the Son of Man [Jesus] be in his day. But first he must endure much suffering and be rejected by this generation." LUKE 17:24–25 NRSV

Prophecied hundreds of years before Jesus' birth, Psalm 22 describes in detail the suffering that Jesus would endure during His crucifixion. Jesus loved us enough to take our penalty and become us, to become our sins. Being our sins is a condition so horrible that He describes Himself as a worm and not a man.

"But I am a worm, and no man; a reproach of men, and the despised of the people."

PSALM 22:6 DARBY

I am poured out like water, and all my bones are out of joint. My heart has turned to wax; it has melted away within me. My strength is dried up like a potsherd, and my tongue sticks to the roof of my mouth; you lay me in the dust of death. Dogs have surrounded me; a band of evil men has encircled me, they have pierced my hands and my feet. PSALM 22:14–16 NIV

Thou hast known my reproach, and my shame, and my dishonour: mine adversaries are all before thee. Reproach hath broken my heart; and I am full of heaviness: and I looked for some to take pity, but there was none; and for comforters, but I found none. They gave me also gall for my meat; and in my thirst they gave me vinegar to drink. PSALM 69:19–21 KJV

This was prophecied hundreds of years earlier by David, describing Jesus' ordeal when He was nailed on the cross, and the Roman soldiers tried to make Him drink vinegar.

Then they spat in his face, and struck him; and some slapped him. MATTHEW 26:67 RSV

Jesus said to them, "My soul is overwhelmed with sorrow to the point of death."

MATTHEW 26:38 NIV

He is despised and rejected by men, a Man of sorrows and acquainted with grief. And we hid, as it were, our faces from Him; He was despised, and we did not esteem Him.   ISAIAH 53:3 NKJV

Jesus' physical condition as a result of this ordeal represented our spiritually sinful condition. He was flogged, beaten, insulted, and humiliated the entire night before He was crucified.

"From head to foot you are sick and weak and faint, covered with bruises and welts and infected wounds, unanointed and unbound."

ISAIAH 1:6 TLB

He was looked down on, and we put no value on him. But it was our pain he took, and our diseases were put on him: while to us he seemed as one diseased, on whom God's punishment had come. But it was for our sins he was wounded, and for our evil doings he was crushed: he took the punishment by which we have peace, and by his wounds we are made well.   ISAIAH 53:3–5 BBE

Then He said to them, "Thus it is written, and thus it was necessary for the Christ to suffer and to rise from the dead the third day, and that repentance and remission of sins should be preached in His name to all nations."

LUKE 24:46–47 NKJV

But if you do right and suffer for it, and are patient beneath the blows, God is well pleased. This suffering is all part of the work God has given you. Christ, who suffered for you, is your example. Follow in his steps.

1 PETER 2:20–21 TLB

Let us run with perseverance the race that is set before us, looking to Jesus the pioneer and perfecter of our faith, who for the joy that was set before him endured the cross, despising the shame, and is seated at the right hand of the throne of God. Consider him who endured from sinners such hostility against himself, so that you may not grow weary or fainthearted.

HEBREWS 12:1–3 RSV

Sufficient

And my God will supply every need of yours according to his riches in glory in Christ Jesus.

PHILIPPIANS 4:19 RSV

Supernatural

"And these signs will accompany those who believe: in my [Jesus'] name they will cast out demons; they will speak in new tongues; they will pick up serpents, and if they drink any deadly thing, it will not hurt them; they will lay their hands on the sick, and they will recover."

MARK 16:17–18 RSV

Our relationship with God is far more important than what we can do as a result of that relationship.

It was now about the sixth hour, and darkness came over the whole land until the ninth hour, for the sun stopped shining. And the curtain of the temple was torn in two.   LUKE 23:44–45 NIV

The seventy returned with joy, saying, "Lord, in your name even the demons submit to us!" He said to them, ". . .See, I have given you authority to tread on snakes and scorpions, and over all the power of the enemy; and nothing will hurt you. Nevertheless, do not rejoice at this, that the spirits submit to you, but rejoice that your names are written in heaven."

LUKE 10:17–20 NRSV

At the moment Jesus died, supernatural things happened.

At that moment the curtain of the temple was torn in two from top to bottom. The earth shook and the rocks split. The tombs broke open and the bodies of many holy people who had died were raised to life.   MATTHEW 27:51–52 NIV

The curtain of the temple was very important. It separated and protected the people, including the priests, from God's presence. God is so holy that if a priest went behind the curtain before he was properly purified, he would die. Jesus made it possible for us to go directly before God, without having to go through a properly prepared human priest and without requiring the protection of the curtain. Jesus is now our direct way to God.

Supreme

[Jesus,] Who is the image of the invisible God, the firstborn of every creature: For by him were all things created, that are in heaven, and that are in earth, visible and invisible, whether they be thrones, or dominions, or principalities, or powers: all things were created by him, and for him: And he is before all things, and by him all things consist. And he is the head of the body, the church: who is the beginning, the firstborn from the dead; that in all things he might have the preeminence. For it pleased the Father that in him should all fulness dwell; and, having made peace through the blood of his cross, by him to reconcile all things unto himself; by him, I say, whether they be things in earth, or things in heaven. COLOSSIANS 1:15–20 KJV

When he presented his honored Son to the world, God said, "Let all the angels of God worship him." HEBREWS 1:6 NLT

Angels are our servants. Angels worship Jesus. Jesus is our Savior. We should worship Jesus, not angels.

And God never said to an angel, as he did to his Son, "Sit in honor at my right hand until I humble your enemies, making them a footstool under your feet." HEBREWS 1:13, PSALM 110:1 NLT

Surprising

"Therefore you also be ready, for the Son of Man is coming at an hour you do not expect."

LUKE 12:40 NKJV

Sympathetic

Come to me, all you who are troubled and weighted down with care, and I [Jesus] will give you rest. MATTHEW 11:28 BBE

For we do not have a High Priest [Jesus] who cannot sympathize with our weaknesses, but was in all points tempted as we are, yet without sin.

HEBREWS 4:15 NKJV

Happy is he that hath the God of Jacob for his help, whose hope is in the LORD his God: Which made heaven, and earth, the sea, and all that therein is: which keepeth truth for ever: Which executeth judgment for the oppressed: which giveth food to the hungry. The LORD looseth the prisoners: The LORD openeth the eyes of the blind: the LORD raiseth them that are bowed down: the LORD loveth the righteous: The LORD preserveth the strangers; he relieveth the fatherless and widow: but the way of the wicked he turneth upside down.

PSALM 146:5–9 KJV

JESUS. . .T

Teacher

Now behold, one came and said to Him, "Good Teacher, what good thing shall I do that I may have eternal life?" MATTHEW 19:16 NKJV

Tempted

This High Priest of ours understands our weaknesses, for he faced all of the same temptations we do, yet he did not sin. HEBREWS 4:15 NLT

For since he himself [Jesus] has now been through suffering and temptation, he knows what it is like when we suffer and are tempted, and he is wonderfully able to help us.

HEBREWS 2:18 TLB

Transformer

Christ gave His life that He might reconcile us both to God in one body through the cross, thereby bringing the hostility to an end.

EPHESIANS 2:16 RSV

"Reconcile" in the original Greek is apokatalasso, *which means to change completely to. Not to come to an agreement, not to meet halfway, not to balance the books, but to change us completely to what God is!*

True

And we know that Christ, God's Son, has come to help us understand and find the true God. And now we are in God because we are in Jesus Christ his Son, who is the only true God; and he is eternal Life. 1 JOHN 5:20 TLB

Then I saw heaven opened and a white horse standing there; and the one sitting on the horse was named Faithful and True—the one who justly punishes and makes war.

REVELATION 19:11 TLB

Trustworthy

"I am placing a stone in Jerusalem that causes people to stumble, and a rock that makes them fall. But anyone who believes in him will not be disappointed."   ROMANS 9:33 NLT

Because, if you say with your mouth that Jesus is Lord, and have faith in your heart that God has made him come back from the dead, you will have salvation: For with the heart man has faith to get righteousness, and with the mouth he says that Jesus is Lord to get salvation. Because it is said in the holy Writings, Whoever has faith in him will not be shamed.   ROMANS 10:9–11 BBE

Truth

Christ did not sin or ever tell a lie.

1 PETER 2:22 CEV

Jesus said to him, "I am the way, and the truth, and the life. No one comes to the Father except through me."   JOHN 14:6 NRSV

Jesus said to the people who believed in him, "You are truly my disciples if you keep obeying my teachings. And you will know the truth, and the truth will set you free." JOHN 8:31–32 NLT

Jesus answered, "You say that I am a king. For this I was born, and for this I came into the world, to testify to the truth. Everyone who belongs to the truth listens to my voice." JOHN 18:37 NRSV

"You [Jesus] have loved righteousness and hated lawlessness." HEBREWS 1:9 NKJV

JESUS. . .U

Unchanging

And, Thou, Lord, in the beginning hast laid the foundation of the earth; and the heavens are the works of thine hands: They shall perish; but thou remainest; and they all shall wax old as doth a garment; and as a vesture shalt thou fold them up, and they shall be changed: but thou art the same, and thy years shall not fail.

HEBREWS 1:10–12 KJV

Jesus Christ is the same yesterday, and today, and forever. HEBREWS 13:8 NKJV

Unearthly

Jesus says about His followers, "They are not of the world, just as I am not of the world."

JOHN 17:16 NKJV

But to all who received him [Jesus], who believed in his name, he gave power to become children of God, who were born, not of blood or of the will of the flesh or of the will of man, but of God.   JOHN 1:12–13 NRSV

Jesus explains to His followers, If you are hated by the world, keep in mind that I was hated by the world before you. If you were of the world, you would be loved by the world: but because you are not of the world, but I have taken you out of the world, you are hated by the world.

JOHN 15:18–19 BBE

For our citizenship is in heaven, from which we also eagerly wait for the Savior, the Lord Jesus Christ, who will transform our lowly body that it may be conformed to His glorious body, according to the working by which He is able even to subdue all things to Himself.

PHILIPPIANS 3:20–21 NKJV

And He [Jesus] said to them, "You are from beneath; I am from above. You are of this world; I am not of this world."   JOHN 8:23 NKJV

Jesus prayed, "And now, Father, glorify me in your presence with the glory I had with you before the world began. I have revealed you to those whom you gave me out of the world."

JOHN 17:5–6 NIV

Unifier

For ye are all the children of God by faith in Christ Jesus. For as many of you as have been baptized into Christ have put on Christ. There is neither Jew nor Greek, there is neither bond nor free, there is neither male nor female: for ye are all one in Christ Jesus.   GALATIANS 3:26–28 KJV

Unimaginable

I pray that you. . .may have power. . .to grasp how wide and long and high and deep is the love of Christ, and to know this love that surpasses knowledge. . . . To him who is able to do immeasurably more than all that we ask or imagine. . ."

EPHESIANS 3:17–20 NIV

Unique

No one has ever seen God. It is God the only Son, who is close to the Father's heart, who has made him known.   JOHN 1:18 NRSV

Unity

"I [Jesus] and My Father are one."

JOHN 10:30 NKJV

"The LORD our God, the LORD is one!"

DEUTERONOMY 6:4 NKJV

See "Unifier."

Unrecognized

Jesus said to them, "I did one miracle, and you are all astonished."   JOHN 7:21 NIV

Jesus answered, "I did tell you, but you do not believe. The miracles I do in my Father's name speak for me, but you do not believe."
JOHN 10:25–26 NIV

Even after Jesus had done all these miraculous signs in their presence, they still would not believe in him. This was to fulfill the word of Isaiah the prophet: "Lord, who has believed our message and to whom has the arm of the Lord been revealed?"   JOHN 12:37–38 NIV

The Jews answered him, "We have a law, and according to that law he ought to die because he has claimed to be the Son of God."
JOHN 19:7 NRSV

He was in the world, and the world was made through him, yet the world knew him not.
JOHN 1:10 RSV

None of the rulers of this age understood this; for if they had, they would not have crucified the Lord of glory [Jesus].

1 CORINTHIANS 2:8 RSV

JESUS. . .V

Victorious

"This man [Jesus], handed over to you according to the definite plan and foreknowledge of God, you crucified and killed by the hands of those outside the law. But God raised him up, having freed him from death, because it was impossible for him to be held in its power."

ACTS 2:23–24 NRSV

"For David says concerning him, 'I saw the Lord always before me, for he is at my right hand so that I will not be shaken; therefore my heart was glad, and my tongue rejoiced; moreover my flesh will live in hope. For you will not abandon my soul to Hades, or let your Holy One experience corruption.' "

ACTS 2:25–28 NRSV

But thanks be to God, who gives us the victory through our Lord Jesus Christ.

1 CORINTHIANS 15:57 NKJV

For whatever is born of God overcomes the world. And this is the victory that has overcome the world—our faith. Who is he who overcomes the world, but he who believes that Jesus is the Son of God?

1 JOHN 5:4–5 NKJV

Vine

"I [Jesus] am the true vine, and my Father is the gardener. He cuts off every branch that doesn't produce fruit, and he prunes the branches that do bear fruit so they will produce even more."

JOHN 15:1–2 NLT

Jesus as the vine is the source of life and goodness. Some of us are the branches that will be cut off because we bear no fruit, and some of us are the branches that will be trimmed clean so that we will bear more fruit.

JESUS. . .W

Way

Jesus told him, "I am the way, the truth, and the life. No one can come to the Father except through me."   JOHN 14:6 NLT

"There is salvation in no one else, for there is no other name under heaven given among mortals by which we must be saved."   ACTS 4:12 NRSV

Willing

For if, when we were God's enemies, we were reconciled to him through the death of his Son, how much more, having been reconciled, shall we be saved through his [Jesus'] life!

ROMANS 5:10 NIV

And behold, a leper came and worshiped Him, saying, "Lord, if You are willing, You can make me clean." Then Jesus put out His hand and touched him, saying, "I am willing; be cleansed." Immediately his leprosy was cleansed.

MATTHEW 8:2–3 NKJV

Sometimes we think that God is not willing to forgive us and make us clean, or not willing to help us, or not willing to be involved with our lives. But He is willing!

"Whoever comes to me I [Jesus] will never drive away." JOHN 6:37 NIV

Wisdom

Christ, in whom are hidden all the treasures of wisdom and knowledge. . .

COLOSSIANS 2:2–3 NKJV

Witness

"This message is from the one who stands firm, the faithful and true Witness *(of all that is or was or evermore shall be),* the primeval source of God's creation."   REVELATION 3:14 TLB

Even now my witness is in heaven, and the supporter of my cause is on high.   JOB 16:19 BBE

"Jesus Christ, the faithful witness, the firstborn from the dead, and the ruler over the kings of the earth. . ."   REVELATION 1:5 NKJV

Wonderful

For unto us a Child is born. . . And His name will be called Wonderful, Counselor, Mighty God, Everlasting Father, Prince of Peace.

ISAIAH 9:6 NKJV

The entire crowd was rejoicing at all the wonderful things that he [Jesus] was doing.

LUKE 13:17 NRSV

This is so you can show others the goodness of God, for he called you out of the darkness into his wonderful light.   1 PETER 2:9 NLT

Word

The one who existed from the beginning. . .the Word of life.   1 JOHN 1:1 NLT

Jesus is God; God's living message.

The Word became flesh and and made his dwelling among us. We have seen his glory, the glory of the One and Only Son, who came from the Father, full of grace and truth.   JOHN 1:14 NIV

I saw heaven standing open and there before me was a white horse, whose rider is called Faithful and True. With justice he judges and makes war. His eyes are like blazing fire, and on his head are many crowns. . . . He is dressed in a robe dipped in blood, and his name is the Word of God.   REVELATION 19:11–13 NIV

Worthy

Therefore, holy brothers, who share in the heavenly calling, fix your thoughts on Jesus, the apostle and high priest whom we confess. He was faithful to the one who appointed him, just as Moses was faithful in all God's house. Jesus has been found worthy of greater honor than Moses, just as the builder of a house has greater honor than the house itself.   HEBREWS 3:1–3 NIV

"You [Jesus] are worthy to take the scroll and to open its seals, for you were slaughtered and by your blood you ransomed for God saints from every tribe and language and people and nation; you have made them to be a kingdom and priests serving our God, and they will reign on earth."

REVELATION 5:9–10 NRSV

JESUS. . .X

Xristos
Greek for Christ.
See "Christ" above.

"He is the Christ, the chosen of God."
LUKE 23:35 NKJV

"We have found the Messiah" *(which is translated, the Christ).*
JOHN 1:41 NKJV

Messiah means Ruler.

Jesus. . .Y

Yearning (for us)

Jesus explains, "Behold, I stand at the door *(of your heart)* and knock. If anyone hears My voice and opens the door, I will come in to him and dine with him, and he with Me. To him who overcomes I will grant to sit with Me on My throne, as I also overcame and sat down with My Father on His throne."

REVELATION 3:20–21 NKJV

JESUS. . .Z

Zealous

To those who sold doves he said, "Get these out of here! How dare you turn my Father's house into a market!" His disciples remembered that it is written: "Zeal for your house will consume me."

JOHN 2:16–17 NIV

Jesus instructs, "As many as I love, I rebuke and chasten. Therefore be zealous and repent."

REVELATION 3:19 NKJV

His authority shall grow continually, and there shall be endless peace. . .He will establish and uphold it with justice and with righteousness from this time onward and forevermore. The zeal of the LORD of hosts will do this.

ISAIAH 9:7 NRSV

Inspirational Library

Beautiful purse/pocket-size editions of Christian classics bound in flexible leatherette. These books make thoughtful gifts for everyone on your list, including yourself!

When I'm on My Knees   The highly popular collection of devotional thoughts on prayer, especially for women.
Flexible Leatherette $4.97

The Bible Promise Book   Over 1,000 promises from God's Word arranged by topic. What does God promise about matters like: Anger, Illness, Jealousy, Love, Money, Old Age, and Mercy? Find out in this book!
Flexible Leatherette $3.97

Daily Wisdom for Women   A daily devotional for women seeking biblical wisdom to apply to their lives. Scripture taken from the New American Standard Version of the Bible.
Flexible Leatherette $4.97

My Daily Prayer Journal   Each page is dated and features a Scripture verse and ample room for you to record your thoughts, prayers, and praises. One page for each day of the year.
Flexible Leatherette $4.97